Five of a Kind

William J. Plummer

Henry Regnery Company • Chicago

Library of Congress Cataloging in Publication Data

Plummer, William J.   1927-
    Five of a kind.

    1. Gambel's quail—Legends and stories.   I.   Title.
QL795.B57P46   598.6'1   76-6276
ISBN 0-8092-8119-8

Copyright © 1976 by William J. Plummer
All rights reserved
Published by Henry Regnery Company
180 North Michigan Avenue, Chicago, Illinois 60601
Manufactured in the United States of America
Library of Congress Catalog Card Number: 76-6276
International Standard Book Number: 0-8092-8119-8

Published simultaneously in Canada by
Beaverbooks
953 Dillingham Road
Pickering, Ontario L1W 1Z7
Canada

To Gela . . .

. . . one of a kind.

We are not so unique
as we should like to believe.

Robert Ardrey, "African Genesis"

Contents

Prologue

It was a Monday morning in February of 1973, everyone had gone off to work or school, and I was all alone in the quiet house—more so than I had been for some time. Two days earlier I had completed my first book, a true story called *A Quail in the Family.* Its principal character was Peep-Sight, a Gambel's quail who had lived freely with us for his entire life.

As I stood at the kitchen sink rinsing out my breakfast dishes, I gazed out into the backyard where Peep had been recently buried, reflecting upon the remarkable four years we had had with him. I smiled to myself, thinking about what an individual he had been and how close we had all felt to him. The depth of understanding and feeling that had existed between us was way beyond the usual attachment to a dog or cat; truly, he had been one of us. Suddenly, a funny thought popped into my mind: "Who *was* he, really?" It surprised me, the notion that the little bird had been more than he seemed; what did it suggest—reincarnation, or a high level of intelligence?

It was not an entirely serious question, of course, but as I drove to work, passing by occasional patches of natural desert, I continued to think about it. Here was a wild creature who had somehow become closely associated with a small element of human society—a family—and who had integrated himself so completely and intimately into it that one could wonder at his status. And yet had Peep-Sight, the ingenuous "house quail," been all that unique, or was it merely a matter of circumstance? Given the right situation, might the same rapport be established with almost any quail or bird or animal? It was a sobering idea at that—perhaps we were already sharing this earth with countless numbers of quietly intelligent creatures, and our response was to ignore, enslave, or slaughter them.

A provocative thought, but not original. Surely it had occurred to many others before me: Konrad Lorenz, Joy Adamson, Jane Goodall, to name a famous few. The idea, however, continued to stay with me, and it was still much in my mind during the summer of 1974 as Wanda and I and the boys began yet another absorbing adventure involving "quail in the family."

1

Decision

I had a little trouble finding Dr. Campbell's address, even though I knew the vicinity well. When the University of Nevada professor told me where she lived, I had recognized the area at once—it was right on my way to work—but it was an undeveloped, sparsely settled side of Las Vegas, and Professor Campbell's family enjoyed a particularly secluded location.

Identifying the inconspicuous mailbox, I parked and went up to their door. Dr. Campbell answered and showed me through to the backyard, where the five orphaned quail were kept in a cardboard box. I observed en route, however, that her household included three small children, three large dogs, and a nearby swimming pool—all known as potential hazards to infant quail!

The baby birds were even younger than I had expected. Down-covered in beige and brown, they had no feathers yet; pins were just forming on their stubby wings. Examining them and discussing the circumstances of their capture, I estimated that the chicks were only a few days old.

They were endearing little creatures, but when Dr. Campbell asked me if I would like to have them, I was reluctant. True, my wife Wanda and I had been thinking recently along just such lines, but we had made no actual preparations. Furthermore, the professor's children were already attached to the chicks, who in turn were accustomed to their handling. Finally, and here was the real rub, we had certainly not contemplated adopting so many. One, yes; perhaps even two, but five—never. Unlike the Campbells, we lived in a well-developed part of town.

1

The problem was not so much that the five baby chicks would represent a major undertaking initially; it was just that if they should all grow to be adults, it would be difficult to accommodate them. Certainly five grown quail could not live free in our house as Peep-Sight had.* We might manage a pair in this way, perhaps, but no more. Of course it was unlikely that many would survive the fifteen weeks to maturity anyway; even two out of five was optimistic. Then too, they wouldn't actually *have* to live-in—we could keep them caged outdoors. This would be satisfactory while they were growing up at least; then we could see how things stood.

As we chatted, my thoughts raced ahead; gradually I found myself getting used to the idea, and before long, five was beginning to seem a reasonable number at that! In due course I agreed tentatively to take them, subject to Wanda's concurrence, and to the Campbell family's reaching a consensus that it would be for the best. We left it at that: they would discuss it and call us with their decision; meanwhile I would have my dialogue with Wanda.

That evening as we talked, we both laughed a little nervously at the prospect. Were we seriously considering the adoption of five baby quail? I kept hearing my words coming back to haunt us:

"Don't do it," I had always said. "It would be a mistake. Aside from the legalities, the day-to-day obstacles are just too overwhelming, the demands too special." As a species, the Gambel's quail is amazingly tenacious, but taken individually, their chances of survival are uncommonly poor. My consistent advice, public or private, had always been simply, "Leave the rearing of baby quail to the professionals—to the game breeders, and to the quail themselves; they know what they are doing." (And still they experience more failure than success.)

People were inclined to listen—I guess we appeared to be experts, having successfully raised Peep-Sight and having published his story. Even in his case, however, we had not set out deliberately to adopt a desert quail; circumstances had thrust this newly hatched Gambel's chick upon us, leaving us no alternative short of abandoning him. Somewhat reluctantly, then, we had accepted the unsought responsibility, and eventually we invested a great deal of patience and concern in determining the little fellow's needs, and in doing our best to meet them. Even so, we felt that it had taken more than our well-intentioned bumbling to enable the tiny chick to grow into a handsome rooster (and full-fledged member of our household); it had required a great deal of good luck as well.

The satisfactions of knowing Peep-Sight had more than repaid us for our trouble. Nonetheless, we felt that few families would wish to commit themselves knowingly to so much bother, especially facing a strong likelihood of failure, and so we advised others against it. I guess we considered ourselves

---

*A Quail in the Family, by William J. Plummer, Henry Regnery Company, Chicago, 1974.

somewhat peculiar in this respect—we had a long history of bringing desert wildlife into our home or yard.

It had begun when we moved to Las Vegas in 1960. We found the place to be as advertised: a remarkable town—Entertainment City—tourism and gambling its primary industries. We lived right in the middle of it, never far from the Strip. Yet, even at the start, we identified with the Nevada desert and its wild creatures instead of the clamoring metropolis. In the midst of all the tinsel and turmoil, we took great pleasure in maintaining our close contact with nature.

Only a few days old, a Gambel's quail is incredibly tiny and fragile, dwarfed by Rob's finger (left) or Wanda's hands (above).

Leslie, our firstborn, was only six years old then; her younger brothers—Chris, Rob, and Mike—followed chronologically at intervals of about eighteen months each. As our four offspring grew, Wanda and I were pleased at their healthy interest in nature and wildlife. We encouraged it, and through the years we helped the children provide housing and sympathetic support for a variety of intriguing desert creatures. We felt that we had all benefited by the involvement.*

It had been a full and interesting time, but it had passed; and now it was 1974. Our animal friends were gone, and the family itself was shrinking. Leslie was no longer six (she and her *husband* were moving to Georgia), and Chris would leave shortly for an Arizona college.

With parental responsibilities diminished, Wanda and I had begun recently to think of taking on an "orphan" or two by ourselves. In early summer, the Peep-Sight book was just out and attracting some attention. It reminded us what fun it had been to watch the captivating little creature grow, and we were considering the possibility of some new, similar adventure. Just to be ready, I had applied to the Nevada Fish and Game Department for a Non-Commercial Breeder's Permit and had checked with a professional supplier on his expected hatch of quail. We had no plans yet, but obviously we were psychologically prepared. The stage was set for what happened next, and it could hardly have been more fortuitous.

I was at the university one morning with a copy of *A Quail in the Family*, and I chanced to meet Professor Campbell, who remarked that she had herself "acquired five baby quail." They had just appeared at her doorstep, and once I learned where she lived, it didn't seem surprising. I called the section "Newton's Corners," a large, undeveloped area surrounding the intersection of Sunset and Pecos roads. On one corner was entertainer Wayne Newton's "Casa de Shenandoah" complete with peacocks, Arabian horses, and fish ponds. The rest was a tangle of mesquite and creosote bush; it sheltered rabbits, roadrunners, pheasants, ground squirrels, and, in great abundance, the Gambel's quail. Except for the growing commerce, it was practically a desert preserve.

Driving by the area during February and March, I had often observed the quail in their large winter coveys; later I noted that they had broken up into smaller groups, which dwindled as many were paired off. Then in May I began to spot an occasional lone rooster perched on a rock or fence post, standing watch while his unseen mate incubated eggs on a nest hidden somewhere nearby. Recently I had seen the first proud parents, emerging finally with their broods of incredibly tiny chicks (and scurrying them off into the rabbit brush when I pulled over for a closer look).

It was too bad, I thought, that this rustic section wouldn't remain unspoiled for long; traffic was already beginning to show a sharp increase. I could readily imagine that a new brood of desert quail, feeding at the edge of this deceptively quiet country road, might be scattered irreparably by the

---

*Friends of the Family, by William J. Plummer, Henry Regnery Company, Chicago, 1975.

sudden passage of a speeding vehicle. Such an episode would be especially disruptive if it came too soon after the chicks had hatched, before they could learn the protective reaction patterns that the skillful parents so quickly set up.

I had suggested this to Dr. Campbell that morning at the university as an explanation for her foundlings; soon I found myself, in my role as "expert," counseling her with regard to their care. Naturally enough, in true professional fashion, I followed up the next day with a call to ask how her wards were faring. She had invited me by to see for myself, and since this was what had been in my mind all along, I accepted quickly.

Thus it was that I came to be looking for the Campbells' difficult address and that Wanda and I found ourselves on a summer evening in 1974 considering an appreciably larger undertaking than we had ever intended.

As we continued our discussion, I began to be excited at the semiscientific aspects of the project. I enjoy learning about behavior patterns, and living with Peep-Sight had provided us with many interesting observations. But we wondered how much of it was typical, and what had been individualistic. Furthermore, Peep had been raised alone—how might he have acted with siblings? Here was an attractive opportunity to make comparisons. It would be fun to watch relative growth and actions, to see individual personalities taking shape, and to take notes and perhaps even draw conclusions. Of course, we said, the birds' welfare would always come first.

It was this latter thought that finally persuaded us—a recognition of our qualifications to determine what was best. We discovered that we had considerable confidence in our own judgment after all. No longer operating from "ignorance and good intentions," this time we had knowledge and experience. Very likely, the birds would be better off now with us than almost anywhere else. We concluded finally that if they were offered to us, we would accept them. There would be problems, certainly, but we would manage. With the matter finally resolved, we went to bed.

Next morning I received the awaited call. One of the chicks had fallen victim to the dogs—the professor's family took this as an omen and voted to give up the birds. She sounded relieved that we would take them, and the matter was quickly settled.

The loss of the chick, while not surprising, disappointed me. I had been charmed by the fuzzy quintet, even at one brief exposure, and I hated losing any of them. Despite the impracticalities of having so many, five had already come to seem the right number.

I was pleased, nonetheless, to have the four survivors, and I picked them up that afternoon on my way home from work. Beaming as I carried the cardboard box gingerly into the house, I announced to Wanda and the boys that we were, ipso facto, Non-Commercial Quail Breeders once again! We laughed and wondered where it would lead this time.*

---

*Lest the reader be misled, a Breeder's Permit does not allow one to remove game birds from their natural habitat. For a discussion of this point, see the Addendum.

2

A Beginning

Wanda and the boys were predictably pleased with our new orphans because it had been a long time since we had seen any so small. Their vigor and verve amazed us anew. Their obvious vulnerability was touching, too, and we resolved that, wherever our new adventure might lead, we would do our best for these little birds, just as we had for Peep-Sight.

Their first need was housing. Since the next day was Friday, we continued to use the cardboard box, planning to find or fashion a suitable home for them on the weekend. One good possibility was the "Meany-olium," a well-fabricated lizard cage that had been with us for many years but which had stood unused in recent times. It was about 3 by 3 by 4 feet, a redwood frame covered with hardware mesh. Although designed for small reptiles, perhaps it could be made suitable for baby quail, at least for a month or so, until they outgrew it. Rob and Mike agreed to check it over the next day.

Meanwhile, after supper Chris was off to the park and the rest of us took our new wards outside to get acquainted. On the lawn, we made a corral of boards to confine the chicks. They were just as enchanting as we had expected—dashing busily about in all directions after infinitesimal insects, tugging at a blade of grass until their huge feet slipped out from under, or scrunching under a leaf to hide from a passing butterfly. Hardly bigger than june bugs, all four could be held in one hand, were it not for their squirming. Large feet and a tiny tuft of topknot were their trademarks.

We had just returned them to their temporary quarters when Chris came back from his outing with an incredible surprise for us—a fifth baby quail!

He had come upon it in an open grassy area where there was clearly nothing else around—the chick was completely alone, lost or abandoned. We chattered in disbelief, not at Chris's story, but at the fact itself. Nothing of the sort had happened to us since Mike had found Peep-Sight five years earlier. It was such a totally unexpected yet appropriate development that we could only marvel at it. Somehow it seemed that we had been here before.

Contemplating the evidence, we agreed that it surely supported what we had so often heard: the first 24 hours after hatchout is a most critical time for baby quail—many then are lost, go astray, or are stolen. I began to wonder how many are adopted!

The newcomer was slightly smaller than the others, about the same size they had been when I first saw them a few days earlier; I judged him to be still in his first day. In any case, with this acquisition the original number had been magically restored. We felt that we were indeed off to a remarkable beginning; now it was time to address other problems.

The next day Rob and Mike reported that the Meany-olium looked promising but in need of repair. They cleaned it up, and on Saturday we put it in good condition. Solidly anchored to the house at a well-sheltered inside corner of the patio, it would do nicely for the chicks once we installed the usual accoutrements: desert sand, rocks, driftwood, and dispensers for seeds and water. Concrete blocks inside held down the corners and formed inviting, cavelike chambers for exploration. Inevitably, too, there was the Christmas light incubator, a veteran of several earlier campaigns. Its main frame was a cigar box; I reupholstered this and mounted it horizontally in a corner of the cage. It was at a suitable height for the chicks to nestle under without danger of being overheated; eventually they could hop up to roost on top.

Before installing our orphans, we paused to photograph them; unfortunately Chris's protege took this opportunity to escape into the yucca patch, which was an ideal hideout. It made him virtually impossible to spot, and the daggerlike leaves guaranteed that he would be unreachable in any case.

We elected not to go in after him but solved the problem instead by placing the other four chicks in a mouse cage at the edge of the patio, invitingly near the yucca. Several hours of watching were rewarded when the Wayward One was finally decoyed out, recaptured, and returned to his new family.

Now at last we placed the five tiny birds in the Meany-olium. It seemed huge by comparison, practically swallowing them up. They appeared not to mind but delighted in discovering its many features. They ate and drank and ran about with great abandon, exploring everything. Although only a few days old, one of them already knew how to scratch with alternate feet like a chicken, and another had actually learned the rudiments of the dust bath (but he got stepped upon whenever he attempted to demonstrate). Both actions seemed comical in creatures so small.

As dusk fell that first night, the entire group was huddled at one end of the cage and paid no attention when I turned on the brooder light. Checking back later, however, I found them all underneath it, soaking up the soft, red glow of the Christmas bulbs.

For the next few days, we set up the temporary enclosure on the lawn each evening, a little corral of boards where the chicks could take their exercise. Despite their size and fragility, they appeared healthy; all showed good ability to jump up to things, fluttering their featherless wing stubs instinctively.

Comfortably ensconced in the Meany-olium, the birds peer out at a "huge" sparrow on the patio (upper). Outside, they are nearly lost in the grass (lower). (Number five is far right.)

Back in the Meany-olium, periods of high activity alternated with frequent naps. To sleep, the whole brood generally piled together, although in the hottest part of the day they preferred to stretch out separately on the rocks or to drape themselves charmingly over a crotch of driftwood. Chris's addition was less domestic than the others, and sometimes kept to himself a short distance away.

Seeing the five so small and helpless, I wondered how these downy "june bugs" had ever managed to make it through their first week of life with its uncertain dangers and misadventures. Presumably they were safer now with us in their sturdy new home; but still they were so vulnerable, and there were a great many hazards. Five little fuzz-balls—how many would make it through another day?

I paused a moment to reflect upon the tremendous odds that the desert quail face daily, merely in maintaining their existence. We had guessed that only one chick in four reaches maturity (some estimates are lower), and the chances of a mated pair surviving intact from one season to the next are probably no better than even. Taken singly, the Gambel's are physically fragile, quite susceptible to injury; yet as a species they manage to demonstrate a remarkable resilience, persistently bouncing back from adverse circumstances to reestablish themselves. I believe that this unusual tenacity can be attributed to three basic characteristics: a fine sensory acuity, a tremendous capacity to learn from experience, and an uncanny ability to adapt, both collectively and as individuals. To me, the Gambel's is one of nature's masterworks; the more I learn of the species, the more I come to admire it.

In raising Peep-Sight, we had commented that the combination of ignorance and good intentions had served us well. We were dealing then with only a single individual, and it was in fact surprising that he had prevailed against such considerable odds. The lesson for us, however, was not one of blind perseverance but something quite different. We had learned that a given objective, if reasonably realistic, can be attained without knowing in advance exactly how each step is to be achieved. A feeling of confidence has value in itself, we found, and specific solutions can wait until they are needed—let intuition and spontaneity have their day! It was with this rather heady philosophy in mind that we had accepted the responsibility for the brood in the first place and with which we now proceeded to the initial phases of our new endeavor.

I decided to keep a journal (the semiscientist emerging). I would record contemporaneously my observations and speculations and compare the development of these birds with the way we remembered Peep-Sight. For reference purposes I needed a date of origin; I arbitrarily set Sunday, June 9, as hatchout day. This was the day before the professor had found the chicks, and I felt confident that it couldn't be more than a few hours off. The exception would be Chris's foundling, whom we now called Red-Leg (having marked him thus with a band of nail polish). The June 9 date probably overstated Red-Leg's true age by a few days, but it seemed a worthwhile concession in order to have a consistent date for all.

On Sunday morning the birds were presumably just starting their second week and, in their sizable world, the Meany-olium, all were active and chirpy. They enjoyed hopping up onto the rocks and blocks and to the lower twigs of the roosting bushes I had installed at each end. Frequently they came to stand under the brooder lights, stretching their necks up toward the warmth. They ate steadily, appearing to relish especially Cream-of-Wheat, the canary seed-tree, and a tender sprig of asparagus fern.

They were far from tame, however, and so in taking them out for their evening exercise we had first the struggle of capturing them. One or another of us would scramble halfway into the cage to corner one chick at a time, placing him in a three-gallon plastic bucket. Once we had collected all five, we carried the bucket out to the back lawn and released them into the temporary corral of boards.

Finding themselves in this enclosure, the birds darted about happily, exploring every corner. We watched, and from time to time we would catch one and hold him for a moment, talking to him softly. Any taming effect that may have resulted, however, was not immediately noticeable.

One day, in fact, the youngster Red-Leg escaped from our jury-rigged corral and dashed to hide in the woodpile. This time we were at a loss to lure him out, and we had to take down the entire stack to recapture the terrified little fellow and return him, bedraggled, to his home.

But if Red-Leg the replacement was still wild, two of the originals (now designated as Brownie and Rose) were gradually becoming tame and attached to us. During exercise they were likely to stay close and look to us for treats. The boys brought them flies and hoppers and, in fact, could call all five to the front of the cage with "To-eat, to-eat."

Brownie and Rose were the most responsive, but all of the birds were beginning to be imprinted upon us (their instincts told them that since we were so often at hand, we must be their parent-companions). When no one was nearby, they might call to us from the Meany-olium: "Peep-peep-peep," continuing until someone appeared to talk to them.

Not surprisingly, after a few days we began to find the evening exercise routine, with its capture, transport, and return, a bit troublesome. As a first step to smooth it out, we set up another corral of boards around the front of the Meany-olium. Now, in returning the birds, we could simply place them in this contiguous enclosure, directed toward the open entrance of their familiar cage. They responded well.

Next we wanted to do away with the corral on the lawn, so one afternoon we tried taking just Brownie and Rose out without it. The experiment worked: Even though unconfined, they stayed close to us, making no move at all to run off. Indeed, when they were frightened by a sparrow or butterfly they came scurrying to us for protection.

Introducing Red-Leg to the same situation, however, produced quite different results. He was still too wild, and so we returned him promptly to the cage. Next came Carrot-Top, or, more familiarly, Carrie, another of the original four (the last was named Pearl). Carrie was frightened too, and eventually managed to escape. This time there was a long, hectic pursuit through the shrubs and flower beds, and when we finally recaptured the truant, he was exhausted and mopey. Plied with flies and small grasshoppers, he soon regained his strength—for the stamina of young quail, there seemed to be nothing so restorative as insects (the chicken soup of the Gambel's world).

The exercise sessions were a great success, but the birds appeared to appreciate the Meany-olium, too. Even while awake, they liked to stretch out in its sand, their necks and legs extended in postures of prostration. In the heat of the day, they stood with featherless wings held away from their bodies, improving the ventilation.

The cool evenings on the lawn were a high point in their day, however, and we continued the regular outings using the corral of boards for a while longer. The chicks were most active here, darting about helter-skelter after little insects, pecking at bits of grit, grass shoots and roots, and the leaves of weeds. Knowing that the young birds need a considerable "animal" content in their feed, we continued to assist by swatting flies and moths for them as we "sat."

In addition, I began buying a few mealworms at the pet store. At first we thought these beetle larvae would be too large for them to handle, but their capacity surprised us. A mealworm was a huge bite for a chick, but turned exactly endwise, it could be gulped down. Surely, we thought, only one such worm will fill so small a belly, but back they came for seconds and thirds and still had plenty of room left for poppy seeds and Instant Ralston!

The chicks' days were full and active, and as dusk fell, back in the Meany-olium, Brownie and Rose would take positions a little way up into the roosting shrubs, yawning and dozing. Soon the others followed, and then all five would be tiptoeing precariously about in the outermost twigs. They would settle down for a while then, looking like diminutive decorations in a miniature Christmas tree; but soon one would get jostled and fall through the spindly branches to the floor and have to work his way up again. Finally, by dark, they were all back together, perfectly still—just a featureless mass of striped fuzz stuck in among the twigs.

Curiously, the chicks often started the morning wild and jumpy, calming down only after their first feeding and nap. It was as though they retained for a while a special wariness that they had assumed to get through the unseen perils of the night; then, as daylight came and visibility improved, they became reassured and relaxed.

As the days passed, the birds, eating and exercising well, thrived and grew. By the second weekend, tail feathers were showing, and their barely formed wing feathers were already effective for short, fluttering hops. We found their activities endlessly interesting and entertaining, and they provided many notes for my journal. Importantly, it seemed, their behavior toward us was reflecting an accommodation: They were less suspicious now, and we could recapture them easily. This made it easier for us to look after their safety.

Then, unexpectedly, we discovered one day that our "june bugs" could actually fly up and out of the plastic bucket; soon these tiny, juvenile birds would have the mobility to fly off on their own. At the moment, they depended upon us for food and shelter, but they might elect at any time to abandon our protection and disappear forever. It hardly seemed possible, they were still so small—and scarcely fourteen days out of their shells!

3

Imprint

Our quintet of quail had been with us for only a brief time, and we knew that we might lose them any day; yet we were encouraged. After all, they were off to a good start in the Meany-olium, and they appeared to be healthy and spirited. In our optimism, we permitted ourselves to consider what we might do if they should actually grow to adulthood. Of course, there would be ample time to work that out during the next three months, but still. . . .

Eventually, we thought, we might select two of them to be our "house quail," as Peep-Sight had been. Perhaps a male and a female—we had often thought of having a mated pair to live-in. Once designated, these two could be slowly introduced to the indoors, then gradually moved into the house for good. As a backup, should anything happen to either of our first choices before they were grown, we could make a replacement from among the others. It sounded a little callous—what would we do with the unchosen birds once all were full-grown? Well, presumably the "understudies" could be released then; they would be less tame, still outdoors-oriented, and should do well on their own.

An interesting idea, but speculative and premature. In any event, we could not begin working toward it yet; there would be no clues as to gender for at least another month. Still, we kept the plan vaguely in mind as we started the third week.

For the time being the chicks were adequately housed and comfortable; we could turn our attention to outside activities. With their increasing mobility, physical constraint was becoming less practical, so it was essential

15

to begin substituting psychological ties to their home territory. We felt this should be done as quickly as possible or we would surely lose them when the first crisis arose. Of course, proceeding too rapidly could be risky, too.

Finally, we took the chance of simply opening the cage and inviting the entire group out. They responded readily, so we led them on into the yard. We were relieved to find that none of them sought to escape—the imprinting instinct was at work telling them that we were their family and that they should stay where we were. Soon we had established the route from cage to yard and return, and we were happy to abandon the bucket and corrals altogether.

This was progress. Before long we could open the door of the Meanyolium and lead the tiny birds right out and across the patio, over to the bed of asparagus fern. Then, as we stayed close by, they would explore up into the Bermuda grass lawn. In no time they were comfortable with this much of their territory, and even in a brisk breeze they would hold together and stay near us.

One day I introduced them to the yucca patch (where Red-Leg had taken refuge only two weeks before); it looked to be a place where they could have fun. They found it scary and unfamiliar but (perhaps consequently) fascinating, and they returned to it often thereafter.

As the quail foraged about on the lawn, curious sparrows sometimes flew down to join them; then little Brownie or Red-Leg, barely half their size, would charge off quixotically to drive the intruders away. When a mockingbird appeared on the wall, however, the chicks would cry out in alarm and run to hide. This was probably well-advised, for the larger mockingbirds are often aggressive about territory.

Each evening, at the end of an hour's outing, our diminutive charges were led or herded gently home. Now, after a relaxing dust bath in the Meanyolium, they would climb up to perch all in a row on an uppermost branch of their "tree." Here they were a charming set, comfortably in repose until someone approached; then they became bright-eyed and alert, like the mice in Disney's *Cinderella*.

Late one night we discovered a cat at the cage—it was Blacky from next door, making the first of what were to be his frequent assaults. Luckily the chicks had been roosting toward the back corner, beyond his reach. We drove the intruder away and checked the cage: it appeared secure. While we were outside the next day, however, I sat cross-legged with a rusty old BB gun in my lap, "riding shotgun" as it were, like a cowboy of the Old West.

The little birds had good wing and tail feathers now and could actually fly the six feet or so up to the top of the wall. Carrie was the first to do so, but he overshot and fluttered into the neighbor's yard (fortunately empty). We could hear the little fellow cheeping, so I scrambled up onto the wall to coax him back, up and over. Eventually he responded, but this time he continued all the way up to our roof. Finally his family called him back down into the yard.

Blacky, the persistent adversary.

Beginning to feel some urgency, I tried to speed up the process of familiarization by taking the chicks out for morning as well as evening sessions. They seemed to appreciate the additional outing. I walked them around the pool and showed them the entire backyard, hoping to enlarge their "home" territory. For the time being, however, I avoided the narrow side yards leading to the front; I didn't want them heading off on their own into these less manageable regions.

Of course, they went anyway. Red-Leg was first to step off (perhaps recognizing the woodpile), and the rest were ready to follow. To distract them, I quickly gave the food call "To-eat, to-eat," and when they came running back I rewarded them with mealworms. Next time they had worked their way around to this same area, I scolded them mildly, then repeated the call and reward, with similar results. After several repetitions it became a pattern, and for many days thereafter, whenever the chicks found themselves at this particular spot on the lawn, they would automatically turn and run back to me to demand their treats! All in all, it seemed a reasonable arrangement, and I saw no reason to object to it.

Moving about in the yard, the little birds occasionally flew, but generally they walked through the grass in a straggly line, their tails up and heads down, somehow reminiscent of lettuce pickers in a California truck garden. Occasionally they would pause and gather to exchange comments on a tasty or exotic weed; then it was back to their harvesting.

We continued to feel that our brood was progressing well. For comparison, I could watch the quail families at Newton's Corners on my way to work—the "real" quail, the boys called them. I saw many now, of various ages. It saddened me to see a pair of adults with only two or three chicks left, but then there were others still with a dozen or more, several weeks old. Often I stopped to observe them from the car for a few minutes, noting relative levels of development and picking up a few pointers on how to be a quail parent (but repressing my urge to get out and compare notes!).

Our five remained healthy and active, almost completely feathered out now, and growing rapidly. They were a family group, but individual personalities were emerging, too. We maintained identification by marking them in various ways with colored ink or nail polish (their names were derived from the original markings), and I scribbled notes daily in my journal. A summarizing entry at the end of three weeks read:

> Rose is currently the most aggressive of the birds, but Brownie, who has become the largest, shows self-confidence too. These are the venturesome two; fearless of us, they take the initiative, often striking out to lead the way off into the unknown. On the other hand, Red-Leg and Carrie are cautious and skeptical, inclined to keep their distance. Pearl, finally, is middle-of-the-road, sometimes accompanying one pair and then again joining in with the other. Much of the time, however, all five are together in a single cluster.
>
> Of the original four, Carrie has the greatest tendency to be a straggler. It is interesting that Carrie clearly prefers the company of Red-Leg, the outsider, who probably became orphaned himself through just such an inclination to lag behind his brood. At the moment, these latter two are the smallest of the five. The explanation in Red-Leg's case may be simply that he is, as we thought, a day or two younger than the others—his plumage development appears to be slightly behind theirs. His progress is good otherwise, though, and while he remains rather independent, he obviously becomes tamer with each passing day.

Actually all the birds were well-established with us by this time—another week had made a considerable difference. Taking stock, we concluded that we had at least lost no ground with them and probably had even gained a little.

But it was not yet time to relax; the critical days were just beginning. These excitable little birds, not yet even sparrow size, were already highly mobile in three dimensions and rapidly increasing their range. When in the yard, they were completely free, and we had practically no control over how they might respond to perceived danger. In any particular case their intuitive reaction could be all wrong for the circumstances, but what could we do to modify it? Their real parents, instinctively wise, would know at once how to direct the entire inexperienced brood into more appropriate behavior. Furthermore, they could do it instantly, with a single, soft syllable, telling their offspring to come together for protection or to run away and hide; to stand perfectly still and motionless or to scatter off noisily in all directions. It was a marvelous, mysterious system of communication, but unfortunately we were not competent in it, and so we would have to devise other means to guide our wards safely through this vulnerable period.

If they could just become familiar with the yard, we thought, and confine themselves to it—or at least return to it quickly when threatened—then we might control and protect the area and thus provide them with a sanctuary. The trick would be in teaching the young quail to recognize and accept these limits. Ideally, they would find that they could be moderately relaxed at home, so long as they remained suspicious of things outside. But this sharp boundary between the refuge of our backyard and the uncertain hazards beyond would be a difficult distinction to make. How could we facilitate their learning in this area or in others?

An important ingredient in the process was their characteristic caution. The chicks instinctively distrusted change; any new aspect to a familiar situation made them uneasy. This reaction could be either a help or hindrance, but it had to be taken into account, as they reminded me one day.

Having decided to provide them a special treat while they were out of their cage, I had dug up a clump of tender grass and placed it in the Meany-olium, thinking to surprise them with a tasty midmorning snack when they returned. Upon seeing it, however, they became instantly apprehensive, reluctant to approach. I suppose it looked to them like some furry intruder in their cage; it didn't belong there, so far as they were concerned. They fussed about it until finally I broke up the clump; then the threat magically disappeared. Now it was only familiar debris, and they ate the roots and shoots with great gusto, just as I had intended they should.

These were suspicious yet venturesome birds, cautious of the unfamiliar, but fascinated by it. Introducing them to desired areas while discouraging the natural inclination to explore beyond was sure to be a challenge. It was an especially hazardous time for them, too—they were still only three weeks old!

Imprinting was not enough. Somehow if I was to look after their welfare I would have to exercise more control over their activities. The first thing I would need was a reliable way to get their attention. Remembering about the pattern at the side yard, it occurred to me that I had already had some success in distracting them with mealworms. Perhaps this was a key.

Mealworms are *Tenebrio molitor,* a common beetle larvae, cultured in wheat bran and sold in pet stores as live food for fish, birds, lizards, and other animals. About ¾-inch long, they are yellowish, segmented, and highly esteemed by young Gambel's quail. That, of course, was the important point. For the next few weeks, mealworms were to be my most useful ally in persuading Brownie, Rose, Carrie, Pearl, and Red-Leg to respond to my protective direction.

4

Mealworms and Machismo

Mealworms can be stored in the refrigerator, alive but dormant, for considerable periods, assuming that the cook will stand for it. After a token reluctance, the Plummer cook agreed, and together we laid in a supply of these beetle larvae to begin our fourth week as Non-Commercial Game Breeders. We hoped they would afford us a measure of control over our rapidly developing quail.

At first I used the mealworms to train the chicks to my knee and shoulder and to establish a general rapport with them. They liked the idea, and before long, during our outings, they would come to me and hop up on my lap unbidden.

One day I coaxed them up to the birdbath, hoping to make them aware of this convenient outdoor source of water. They tromped around in it for a while, slightly uneasy at wetting their feet; then one of them discovered its potability, and they all paused in their play to enjoy a refreshing drink. It was a huge success, and thereafter they flew up often for that purpose.

Another time I suggested that they hop up to the top of a lava boulder near the yucca patch—it looked like a logical place for them to sun for a moment or just to look around. Again they followed readily, posing in a picturesque group. They liked the spot and began using it as a regular stopover to and from their outings.

When I thought about it, I was surprised at how well the chicks appeared to understand what I had in mind and how often they complied with my direction, even in the absence of the mealworm incentive. I didn't speak

21

their language but they seemed to sense my meaning intuitively.

When I held out my hand and asked them to jump up, or to go somewhere, they usually did so. I didn't understand it—surely I must have looked to them like nothing but a cumbersome giant, gesturing in the grossest fashion, and yet more often than not they would hop up to this, or proceed to investigate that, just as I had wished, leaving me to wonder how they had ever managed to fathom my intent.

Next I encouraged them to explore further the interesting protected areas in the yucca patch itself and in the concrete planters nearby, hoping that these would become familiar to them as potential hiding places (Blacky the cat, or a small dog, might slip into the yard unexpectedly at any time). As before, they responded well. When I began leading them occasionally on a tour around the pool, however, they looked at me questioningly. They followed, but this time it seemed as though they were humoring me and did not place much value on the excursion themselves.

After one morning outing, Wanda and I enticed the brood into the family room. Here, with the help of the mealworms again, we introduced the birds to the elevated hearth, the windowsill, the couch, and chair. A little wary at first, they adapted quickly, flying to the lamp and the traverse rods and generally demonstrating interest and acceptance.

That evening we were surprised to see an effort at control of the group originating in another quarter (but without the help of mealworms). It was Red-Leg, the presumed junior member of the family, behaving in an unexpected way. As dusk approached, there was a collective indecisiveness about roosting sites; the chicks moved about restlessly, trying for some time to reach consensus on a suitable spot. Finally, Red-Leg appeared to lose patience with the whole procedure. Systematically and in turn, he pecked each of the others severely on the head, just once, then settled himself onto an appropriate roost. Apparently he succeeded in making his point, for shortly thereafter the entire group had joined him in what was clearly to be the night's sleeping location.

The incident drew our attention again to Red-Leg, and we noticed that he had caught up to the others physically—he no longer appeared smaller or younger. Furthermore, although he remained the independent spirit, he was becoming something of a leader; often now the others would come to him rather than vice versa.

Actually, each of the birds continued to develop his individual personality, yet all retained a strong group identity. The Campbells came by one day to see the brood, and they asked whether any reminded us particularly of Peep-Sight. I found it a difficult question to answer. Collectively, yes, but individually I could hardly think about one of them by himself, without relating him to the group as a whole. They were already becoming an entity.

Perhaps it would be Red-Leg, I thought—his independence and his appearance were both reminiscent of Peep. On the other hand, there was Carrie, the cautious skeptic, whose increasing interest in safety and security was also characteristic of his predecessor. Then Brownie reflected that strong "people-orientation" that we had seen from the beginning; and Rose was much the same—she had lost her agressiveness and liked to hang around her human "parents" waiting for a handout. Pearl did so too, but somehow both she and Rose seemed feminine, whereas Peep-Sight had always projected a definite machismo.

The thought led me back to the question of gender. It was still too early to tell which of the birds was of which sex, but we continued to conjecture on the matter. Probability suggested that we would have two of one sex and three of the other—in poker terms, a Full House. Watching their behavior and growth, I decided to go on record, just for fun, and predict that Brownie, Carrie, and Red-Leg were males, while Rose and Pearl were females. Of course it was purely a guess. Sex-related color variations should show up in another few weeks and then it would be apparent how close I came.

Meanwhile the birds were fully feathered except for their fuzzy topknots. In general their feathers were larger than body size required; it was not a particularly appealing stage in their development. For the moment, they had that ungainly look of little turkeys. Actually, at four weeks, they were still not as large as the sparrows!

At the end of a month, the chicks are far from charming—they look like ungainly little turkeys!

Nevertheless, I was surprised one day to notice how much they *had* grown. Driving to work, I discovered that a familiar pair of "real" quail, whom I thought not to have mated successfully, were apparently only late, for here they were now, proudly leading a dozen or more chicks forth on what must have been their first day's foray. I was amazed to see how small their babies were; *our* youngsters were large by comparison.

I didn't envy those new parents the task of getting their tiny brood safely through the next three or four weeks; that much, at least, was successfully behind us. It had been hectic; but what we were beginning next would be exciting too.

Our birds took to the air regularly now during their outings, from one corner of the lawn to the other. And, at any uncommonly loud sound, they might scatter noisily in all directions, off to the walls and trees. We were encouraged, however, to see that they began contacting each other immediately afterward, re-collecting into a covey at home.

In reassembly, the call is the most important factor. Toward the end of the fourth week we had noticed a significant change in voice: the regular peeping had become a metered "Peep-peep, peep-peep, peep-peep." It was the beginning of adolescence, we thought, and the first step toward the adult "Chuk-CAW, chuk-CAW-caw!" Now, sure enough, as another week started, we heard Brownie and Red-Leg making their first rasping attempts at the mature calls, and within a few days the entire brood was croaking at each other whenever they became separated. Fortunately the birds typically limited their dispersions to short range, so there was no occasion for panic; meanwhile, the whole procedure was good practice for them.

It was obvious that the group was becoming relaxed, beginning to establish its territorial limits inside the yard, just as we had hoped. With growing familiarity we all felt more secure, especially the surrogate parents. One evening, when our little birds scattered off into the neighbors' yard on both sides, we were pleased to see that our earlier efforts and the practice sessions were paying off—they all returned promptly and without incident. It was smooth and reassuring.

We were enjoying our wards; and we were pleased to see that, along with their high spirits, they appeared to be maintaining excellent health. They continued to grow rapidly, eating alyssum, marigolds, moths, Ritz crackers, poppy seeds, radish tops, and of course, mealworms. (Eventually Peep-Sight's favorite, cherry-pie filling, took its rightful place as well.)

During the fifth week there were suggestions of changes to come. Brownie grew colorful russet side feathers, and when we looked more closely, Red-Leg and Carrie were developing them, too. They were not yet evident on Rose and Pearl. Soon we would see the basic differences and know how to proceed.

With full plumage, preening and dust baths became popular. This latter activity is important to the birds as soon as their feathers appear, becoming a part of their daily routine. Its purpose is to clean and massage the skin, to brush and stimulate the feathers, keeping them free of vermin, and to cool the body on hot days. Apparently it has considerable recreative value as well, for they obviously find it highly pleasurable. Our young quail had not yet developed it into the typical elaborate ritual, but they clearly enjoyed it and indulged frequently in communal dust baths. Each participated happily in the shower of dirt thrown up by the others, like children splashing together in a backyard pool.

As the fifth week drew to an end, it was time to give the Meany-olium a good cleaning. While Wanda kept the birds occupied in the family room, Chris and I stripped everything out and cleaned it up, providing new sand and fresh foliage; then we reinstalled the key trees, rocks, and shrubs. Of course we couldn't get everything back exactly as it had been, so there was much fuss and suspicion when the birds were asked to reenter this *strange* place! After a while they consented to return, but for a day or two thereafter they were awkward in moving about among the branches—apparently even the placement of these had become familiar to them, and slight variations in position caused them to make false steps.

One day I noticed again that the chicks had grown; they were finally sparrow-size, and big enough to begin crowding the Meany-olium. Surely it couldn't be only a few weeks since it had seemed such a huge arena for them—suddenly it was too small! For the time being, I tried to compensate again by giving them more time outside.

The outings had developed into a regular routine, and the quail had become accustomed to it (as had I). Each morning before work I would open the cage door and invite them out for a stroll. They were ready and eager, and if it was reasonably quiet the little birds trooped calmly out, off the patio and over to the edge of the yucca patch, then up onto the large black lava rock that had become their staging point. Here they would pause in a grouping atop the rock, getting their bearings for a moment and surveying the yard for possible dangers. Satisfied, they would charge off then to attack their favorite alyssum plant, an unfortunate volunteer that had established itself nearby, just below the flower beds. The chicks devoured its seeds, blossoms, and leaves indiscriminately (eventually the poor thing gave up and died, but they continued the ritual until only a few dry twigs remained). Having enough of this, suddenly one of them would streak off across the grass to the farthest corner of the lawn, and the others would flurry and flutter noisily after, as though dramatizing the importance of the move. Here they all piled into a sunny corner, spreading out their limbs languorously to bask in the early morning sunshine, appearing to go instantly to sleep.

In a few minutes, however, they would be up and around again. One might reach up then to pull at a leaf filled with water (from the sprinklers), and soon all were doing it, splashing each other in a sort of family shower. Finally they would be off to police the grass and flower beds.

On windy mornings, or when there was too much noise in the neighborhood, the routine did not proceed so smoothly. It might start out the same, but before all five were out of the cage one or two would take off in a whir; and then the entire group would blast out on a curving path around the corner of the house, out of sight momentarily, then plop directly into the sunny flower bed. The birds were fond of this cozy corner; it was protected from the wind, and on such days they remained close to it to graze.

When the time came for me to go to work, I began walking back toward the patio, and they followed along behind. Usually I could move them at a moderate pace, reversing the original routine of the flower beds, the alyssum, and the lava rock; but if time was short I would go directly to the cage. Once they were inside, there would be a cursory scratching through the seedbox; then they would retire up to a roost for their morning siesta. Dozing in a tight little line, Red-Leg preferred to bury his head under a wing, Pearl let hers droop forward, and the others simply closed their eyes.

Aside from their sleeping postures, the birds' individual characteristics showed in a variety of other ways, too, and these continued to shift (to preserve identities, we renewed their markings from time to time). Pearl and Red-Leg had become confident and self-assured like Brownie, but Rose had turned reticent and was more likely to take alarm. Then there was cautious Carrie, always the skeptic, always warning of possible danger, and last to fly up to the birdbath or to a new rock. Carrie's temperament was always most consistent.

In general, however, the birds were becoming comfortable and relaxed together, and with us. It had been another productive two weeks—the mealworms had helped. We had achieved a degree of control while the chicks continued to develop. Still, a critical period would last for some time longer—the quail had not yet learned the limits of their yard or how to avoid the dangers beyond it.

5

Interlude

As quail "parents," we took great pride and pleasure in watching our offspring develop. Sometimes we became so preoccupied with the gravity of our responsibility that we almost forgot to have fun at it. Not so with the quail themselves; they knew instinctively of the need for recreation. Once we discovered how they played together, watching them became a source of considerable enjoyment for us as well.

With our juveniles entering their sixth week, we were mildly excited at the prospect of learning which were males and females and how close my prediction might come. The prominent difference in marking among adult Gambel's is the cock's russet cap and his distinctive black mask and bib (a black streak across his lower abdomen is less conspicuous). These identifiers show clearly at maturity, but even at six weeks a strong suggestion of them is often detectable in the young roosters.

We were disappointed, however, for in our birds none of the colorful male features had materialized. The most evident variation was still in the streaks of russet on their lower front sides, noticeably brighter on Red-Leg and Brownie. Since this marking is common to adults of both sexes, the difference was of little value for our purpose. With no further evidence I continued to think in terms of a "Full House," i.e., Red-Leg, Brownie, and Carrie as males, and Rose and Pearl as females. It was still entirely intuitive, of course; I hoped that another week or so would bring us the true answers.

But markings or not, the birds were definitely maturing; their calls were smoother now, close to the adult sound and a long way from the peeping of only a week or two ago. On the other hand, first topknot plumes were barely started, and I noted also that side feathers were still "single," i.e., only one feather per pin, rather than the double variety which I knew that adult quail produce.

Meanwhile we found it interesting to note in Red-Leg's appearance the evidences of a different parentage. While the other four, presumably true siblings, were all slim and sharp-faced, Red-Leg the outlander was compact, rounded, and closer to the ground. We could identify him quite readily, whereas with the others we had to look for the ink or nail polish markings to be sure.

We thought that the birds recognized these differences, too. Sometimes they seemed to peer intently at each other; and once, after Carrie had been re-marked (on the head), each of the others came up to study him carefully. One or two attempted to peck the orange ink off his face (but he rejected this impertinent treatment). We felt that they almost certainly used facial recognition among themselves, and probably on us as well.

Appearances changed rapidly, however, for the quail were growing fast—they were five healthy, thrifty birds. By the end of the sixth week they looked to be as large as robins, although much of their size was only fluffed-out plumage. Proportionately, their heads seemed too small, tail feathers too long, and their feet and legs excessively large. Despite all this they were charming characters, and we did not notice any of the awkwardness of movement that had been characteristic of Peep-Sight's intended, the adolescent Lady Bird.

It was at about this time that we came upon what we believed to be a fascinating discovery (the first fruits of my semiscientific approach). We became convinced that the juvenile quail had evolved a regularized play behavior quite like that of young mammals. To us, at least, it was a revelation. There had been flashes of playfulness before, but this appeared to be much more than that—evidently a loosely structured game.

In the beginning, we didn't even recognize it as play. We saw the chicks behaving in a way that we found amusing, but we assumed that it was serious to them. The basic activity looked like an instinctive pattern of evasion against predators, probably from the air. It consisted mainly of darting about in frenetic zigzags, with sudden stops and starts and changes of direction. Interspersed would be frequent "freezes" in a special scrunched down, forward-tilted position, facing outward with head and breast resting on the ground, rump and tail pointed skyward (the invitational posture of a playful puppy?). Then in a few seconds it was "off we go again," fluttering and veering in a dizzying blur. We did think it curious that even a passing butterfly might start this action, or that sometimes one of the birds himself appeared to initiate it; but at first we simply watched and chuckled, saying that they were playing Spooky Quail.

After a while, it occurred to us that perhaps we *were* seeing a form of play. Observing it with this in mind, we were able to find considerable support

At six weeks the half-grown quail bask in the morning sunlight at the corner flower bed (upper); reconnoiter the sky from atop their favorite lava rock (lower).

for the idea. For one thing, the birds did not appear genuinely alarmed at all; they actually seemed to be enjoying themselves. It was as though they really were playfully "spooking" each other, just as our whimsical name suggested. (Wanda thought they were like children out on a dark night, frightening one another just for the thrill of it: "Boo!" "What was that?").

Their responses were a clue, too, for these differed from the authentic frightened reactions that we had come to know. When one of them actually *did* spot possible danger, at his first warning all would freeze instantly, motionless for a minute or more, heads cocked and squatting low (but not in a tail-up position). This reaction was clearly different from the play behavior, both in character and intensity.

When the birds were small, their sport had had little structure, consisting of no more than a general scurrying. Sometimes we referred to it then as the Mouse Game, noticing that their pitter-pattering, as they zipped about among the dry leaves under a euonymus or mock orange, was like the rustling of mice—the covert crackling apparently enhanced the "spooky" effect. Growing up, the quail began to engage in the activity more openly and virtually at every outing, often upon release from the confinement of their cage. This was when we began to suspect that there was more to the action than simple spooking. It had come to resemble a children's game of tag or hide-and-seek. Perhaps, we thought finally, it actually *was* a rudimentary sort of game.

We remembered that the play behavior of young mammals is typically modeled after corresponding adult activities; it is thought to be the instinctive way in which energetic juveniles utilize their high spirits to acquire and practice important skills needed in maturity. Lion cubs, for example, spend much of their time stalking, chasing, and brawling with each other, acting out the behavior of predators and competitors in the jungle. And while they obviously enjoy it immensely, up to a point they perform with great seriousness.

The quails' Mouse Game appeared to be consistent with this. The initiating bird seemed to play the role of predator—a hawk or fox, attempting to frighten the others. With wings outstretched and head down, he would make a sudden threatening charge in their direction, veering off at a sharp angle just before contact. At this point he appeared to switch roles, suddenly dropping his fierce demeanor to become another fluttering member of the "alarmed" covey. All would dart about for a few seconds, eventually freezing in the playful puppy position, head down and rump up. Then, in a moment, another bird might take his turn as predator (was he "it"?) and start the whole thing off again.

As the quail gained mobility, we saw the game develop further and assume refinement. Now one might start it by flying at the others out in the open, a few inches off the ground. When they really got going, often one of them would leap suddenly a foot or two straight up into the air, then drop onto the others in a fair impression of a diving raptor. We began then to refer to it as The Hawk Game, or Hawk and Quail,—the name seemed more descriptive (and comparable to our Fox and Geese).

By this time we were quite convinced of the basic nature of the activity, and naturally we tried to remember whether Peep-Sight growing up had ever demonstrated it. At first we thought not (how could an only child learn to play Fox and Geese?). Then, yes, we recalled having noticed it—not while he was immature, but much later, during the period of his association with the half-grown Lady Bird. At the time, we had certainly not viewed it as playfulness but simply as another of his ways to evade her unwelcome approaches. Recalling it now, however, we agreed that it *had* actually been the same. We concluded that the presence of this adolescent chick had probably elicited a latent playfulness in the crusty old bachelor, causing him to regress momentarily to her juvenile level (not entirely unprecedented behavior, after all, in our human society!).

Five young maids on their morning stroll—from the left: Rose, Pearl, Red-Leg, Carrie, and Brownie.

Whatever the explanation, at the end of their sixth week our birds were full of pep and ginger. Just as significant, perhaps, was their size, for they were about half grown now and the Meany-olium could not serve them much longer. We cleaned it out again, but this time we kept rearrangements to a minimum, and with their growing self-assurance they had little difficulty about reentry.

It was obvious that the quail were increasingly confident of themselves and their situation. Their play behavior reflected a generally bold outlook: *They* felt they were ready for anything. Perhaps they were; the rest of us, however, still held a few reservations.

6

Aviary

Although our primary concern was the birds' safety, we were increasingly uncomfortable about their cramped quarters. The quail were growing rapidly, and while my ideas for expanding their accommodations were crystallizing, I made further efforts to maximize their time outdoors.

We were particularly apprehensive though, because when the birds were out for exercise now their self-confidence was likely to send them off exploring out of sight. Their forays didn't last long—they were ready to flee in an instant—but in nearly every session some of them ended up on the walls or roof. Often several would be strewn out along the top of a neighbor's fence, with perhaps one over on the opposite side. It made us anxious, but so far we were lucky; there had been no dog or cat lying in wait, and after a few minutes the birds had reconvened in our yard. Happily, too, none had gone yet over the forbidden back wall, to contend with the nearby street and its traffic.

We appreciated our good fortune, but we expected that it couldn't last. Our birds were adolescents, and we felt the usual anxieties and frustrations of any parent with teen-agers—heavy responsibility and little control! As with human children, all we could do was caution our wards, be alert, and keep our fingers crossed.

While we philosophized about these similarities, Carrie flew into a window pane and was dazed for a few hours (but then good as new). Another morning, as I sat in the center of the Bermuda lawn, a sudden loud noise frightened two of the birds, who took off simultaneously from opposite corners, each heading directly at me! When I ducked, they collided in mid-air, just a few feet off the ground. Fortunately it was a glancing blow, and except for losing a few feathers neither seemed any the worse for it.

There were other dangers. The mockingbird who included our yard in his territory still came by occasionally to check up on us. Although he remained aggressive, the chicks had grown at least as large as he and he was no longer a serious threat. Still, we wondered what he was up to when we saw him maneuvering on the walkway in a peculiar hopscotch, bouncing along with his wings partially extended, as though hexing us with some sinister ritual.

The weather, too, provided us with a few surprises. An infrequent nocturnal thunderstorm would keep the birds wide-eyed and awake, but they managed to get through the night without undue distress. One morning after a heavy rain they found all sorts of delectable goodies in the grass. Red-Leg, spotting a place where many small angleworms were squirming out of the soil, called the others over, and soon they were all rushing about happily, sharing in the discovery like children at an Easter egg hunt. The moist lawn served to remind us, too, how much these little bipeds used their tails—as tripods while standing and as rudders when they darted about—for soon there were five soggy sets of tail feathers, damp and bedraggled from the wet grass.

Apparently the rain brought out the "real" quail as well. I had not noticed any on my way to work for several weeks; I assumed that they were keeping to cover now, less active in the heat of the day. On this morning, however, as I pulled up to Newton's Corners, I looked over to see a brood of ten, somewhat younger than ours, near the side of the road. As their anxious father nervously brought up the rear, they streamed across a small clearing to the mesquite on the opposite side. I marveled to see that so many had survived the increasingly heavy traffic (which, I thought, probably accounted for the absence of a mother hen). Then I noticed that several of the chicks were smaller than the others—it was not one brood after all, but two. Apparently it was a merging of families to accommodate orphans—and this lone, harassed rooster was the sole surviving parent. One could only guess which group of chicks he had actually fathered (not that it would matter to him). It was another grim reminder of the odds faced by the Gambel's, and the extraordinary adaptability that he typically brings to bear against adversity.

Given the opportunity, I studied these youngsters carefully, looking for differences in coloration, but I detected no more variation among them than I could see at home. I remained as unsure as ever.

But gender notwithstanding, our happy (though tenuous) success continued, and we felt that it made sense for us to consider again what we might do eventually with four or five *adult* quail. While not abandoning our earlier idea of a mated pair living-in, we thought now of the alternative of keeping the entire family permanently in the backyard. Once they were mature, they would surely settle down, and perhaps with the right cage a group of grown birds could be kept safe and secure at home, yet free to come and go as they chose. Of course, if they began ranging far beyond, there would be problems to face. We didn't minimize these; but, consistent with our basic philosophy, we deferred them for later consideration.

We could *not* defer for much longer, however, the problem of larger quarters. My plan had finally taken shape, and so on the weekend I made a trip to the desert, then to the lumberyard, to collect materials for the project. What I had in mind was the construction of a completely new enclosure—a large, airy, protected living space—to replace the Meany-olium, in the very same corner of the patio. It would be an actual aviary of sorts, quite grand.

Building the cage would take considerable effort, but the real problem would be in making the transition. How could I get these cautious birds to transfer from one home to another? Simply interchanging them would surely cause trauma; our entire routine was based upon their identification with the Meany-olium. I could not be optimistic about getting them to accept a totally new, strange enclosure.

I decided to proceed with the project slowly, giving careful attention to detail, and looking for opportunities to acquaint the birds with the new cage, bit by bit. I could spend a week or two building the platform floor, for example, working on it on the patio within their view until it was just right. The birds could be invited to inspect my progress on their way to and from outings; they might fly up and explore it. Next I would make two large side panels, to complete enclosure of the patio's interior corner. By the time I was ready to make the swap, the main parts of this new cage would be already familiar to them.

With the Meany-olium becoming too small, the new, roomy aviary is constructed. (Photos by Wanda Plummer)

It seemed a good plan, and so on Sunday I undertook some preliminaries, using the desert driftwood to fashion a handsome set of natural roosts high up in the corner above the present cage. All the activity and the falling bark disturbed the birds, but they were also immensely interested, eyeing the installation appreciatively. Soon they were flying against the roof of the Meany-olium, trying to get through to these attractive new perches.

For the next couple of evenings, however, they were reluctant about reentering the cage, and I assumed that the driftwood suspended directly above made them cautious. Finally one evening they would not reenter at all, but retreated instead from the patio, making a few nervous passes at Spooky Quail, then skittering about uneasily. Even mealworms availed us nothing. Dusk was falling rapidly, and we were becoming anxious. The five quail clustered on a small, low patio table, contemplating the cage but refusing to go inside.

Then with a sudden, unexpected whir they exploded in all directions. When the dust and feathers had settled, Brownie was in the cage, and two others were on the patio roof. They came down readily and we coaxed them in with Brownie; but we could neither see nor hear the remaining pair. We had no idea where they had gone, and it was nearly dark—where should we look?

We climbed to the roof and walked the walls calling for them, and searched with flashlights in the shrubs and flower beds. Finally, Wanda flashed her light up into the corner at the new roosts above the Meany-olium, and sure enough, there were Red-Leg and Pearl, settled in snuggly on the uppermost branch. The problem, apparently, had not been caution at all, but ambivalence! Having attained their goal, Pearl and Red-Leg remained now as quiet and inconspicuous as possible. They looked so comfortable and secure that we decided to leave them there overnight; early next morning I talked them down into the cage for their breakfast.

I concluded, however, that I had better take the afternoon off to work on the new enclosure—the way things were developing, my leisurely building schedule had to be revised and accelerated. I decided to do the side panels first and, by pressing Rob and Mike into service, had them completed by evening. Then I fabricated the bottom platform (but in the garage), with all the dispatch I could muster. By Saturday afternoon everything was ready.

While the boys "quail-sat" in the family room, Wanda and I quickly ripped out the Meany-olium and all its accumulated mess. We swept and hosed the patio clean; then we installed and secured the bottom platform, replete with lava rock, driftwood, and appropriate bits of foliage. We added a new water dispenser, a bin-type feeder, and a large built-in tin filled with bathing dust. Finally we hooked the side panels into place and made a few adjustments, and there it was—the aviary resplendent, ready for occupancy.

The birds were not impressed. My well-laid plans, of course, had gone for naught—the cage was totally new to them. First of all, they would not set foot on that transparent, alien floor. Instead they flew up directly to the now-familiar roosts, where they panted and complained, moving awk-wardly about from branch to branch. They jostled each other and slipped off and generally dramatized how put-upon they were by the whole tawdry affair. Furthermore, they steadfastly refused to come down, even when I laid newspapers on the floor to give it a look of solidity.

As it grew dark the birds became more and more agitated; the situation was beginning to look irretrievable.

At last Carrie relented and dropped down. He explored for a few minutes in his cautious, long-necked way, until finally he was satisfied. Then sud-denly, as though by a signal, the other four fluttered down to join him, be-ginning immediately to chatter and eat ravenously from every available facility. The crisis was over.

Of course, as expected, there continued to be a few problems. For a while, getting the chicks in and out of their new home involved much cajoling and patience—everything was still too strange. Slowly, however, they began to accept the aviary and, as the ninth week began, the transition appeared to be succeeding.

Inevitably, we paused again to reflect upon our situation. We were still doing well, we thought, but I was becoming uneasy about Carrie, or rather about his influence. Like Peep-Sight, he had elected himself as guardian of the common welfare. However, Carrie was much quicker to give the alarm and took his role most seriously. Outside especially he was the essence of vigilance; his whole demeanor was that of the sentry: watchful, dedicated, alert. Even during dust baths in the protected flower beds, he would post himself a foot or so away, obviously on guard duty. And as the others bustled about on their mundane activities, here was Carrie pausing for a long, motionless moment to study some remote speck in the sky or listening intently to the barely audible bay of a distant hound.

Perhaps, I reasoned, in the wild a covey might owe its survival to just such a super-cautious member as this. Yes, in thinking about it more care-fully, I decided it was reassuring to have Carrie in the group. We needed him: His extreme sensitivity to any change in the surroundings, or to the presence of potential predators, was sure to be an asset. When they eventu-ally undertook explorations beyond our yard, as they certainly would, the welfare of the brood might well depend upon the timely admonitions of a cautious Carrie.

In any case, watching him now as he posed alertly on a bough in the new aviary, I became aware of the tremendous task we had cut out for ourselves in raising these five orphan quail in our modest backyard. Somehow I was reminded again of the problems of raising children in today's environment. One cannot keep them locked up and protected indefinitely in a comfortable "cage" or even hope to buffer them in any important degree from the dangers and temptations of the world. One can only give them as much freedom and room to grow as possible, offer guidance and affection, and trust that they will somehow manage to get through the attractive distractions of adoles-

cence. Yet, for the human temperament, raising them singly is surely challenge enough. Trying to cope with an entire brood all at once seemed almost
an impossible task!

*Once accustomed to the new home, Red-Leg claims an upper roost (left), but there is
plenty of room for all five adolescent quail.*

7

Carrie Cuts Out

Getting the birds transferred from the outgrown Meany-olium into their fine new aviary kept my attention for a couple of weeks, and I had hardly thought about the annoying question of gender. Now, however, we found ourselves awakening in the mornings to the sound of the calling quail—the roomy new cage seemed to encourage them—and I would sometimes listen for distinguishing vocal characteristics. For a moment I might identify the caller as probably a male or female; then suddenly I would remember: I had no basis yet for making such distinctions. As the "expert," I felt a little embarrassed. The birds, after all, were starting their *tenth* week; by this time we should know something of their sexes.

Waking to the quail calls was great fun, reminiscent of camping out. They began about 6:30, just outside the kitchen door, "Chuk-CAW-caw!" All five had mature voices now; Rose had been the last to lose the raspy, croaking sound. There were distinct vocal variations developing all right, but I heard no particular pattern that might correlate with gender.

Nothing had happened to change my original prediction: Pearl and Rose (fortuitously named) were females; the other three were males. For now, it still seemed as good a guess as any.

Meanwhile, summarizing the notes in my journal, I reviewed their personalities, which were developing consistently in some respects but erratically in others.

Red-Leg continues to be the most independent, and with his rapid physical development he has surpassed the others in size. Interestingly, he and Pearl, the

41

daintiest of the group, show signs of a special affinity. We can't resist thinking ahead to the possibility of their pairing off (noting their separate parentages).

Pearl and Brownie have become great beggars, hanging around their sitter, jumping to a knee or shoulder to solicit treats. Brownie, however, despite his tameness and easy capture, sets up a horrendous outcry whenever he is held, as though claiming all kinds of abuse and privation!

It is interesting that each of the quail seems to have his turn at undergoing a "jumpy" period. Initially it was Red-Leg—inclined to take alarm and dash off at any loud noise or unexpected movement. After a few weeks he became more relaxed, even poised and confident, although retaining his aloofness.

Then it was Carrie, developing a characteristic penchant for vigilance; for several weeks he seemed to initiate nearly every episode of scattering. But Carrie, too, has calmed down and is more discriminating in his "wolf"-crying (though he still performs as the official lookout).

Now it is Pearl who appears to be suffering through a general uneasiness; she is last to come down for feeding, overly cautious and likely to fly off irrationally. And it is Pearl, from some elevated perch, who occasionally calls out to precipitate a general alarm, at nothing more apparent than a quick movement or a loud sound.

I wondered whether we could expect next to see similar regressions by the steadfast Rose and Brownie, or whether, as I thought, they had already experienced their turns in milder form. I hoped we had, for despite my optimism at what appeared to be initial acceptance, the new cage was causing a series of disruptions in our routine, and for a time we seemed to go from one minor crisis to another.

I suppose instability was inherent in the circumstances. The birds were changing so fast that one could hardly expect to predict their behavior. What was familiar and acceptable to them one day was threatening the next, and today's off-limits would be the site for tomorrow's exploratory expedition.

In any case, getting the quail to leave the cage or return more or less at my direction, as they had done with the Meany-olium, was turning out to be difficult. Several factors seemed to be involved. One was the elevated platform—as the birds approached to enter, they could not see their familiar furnishings and were reluctant to fly up to it. It helped when I provided them an intermediate step, so they could hop up and survey the interior before venturing in.

Another difficulty was the deceptive aspect of the "see-though" hardware mesh that constituted the floor; they considered it untrustworthy and spent much of their day roosting near the roof to avoid stepping upon it. Unfortunately their reaction maximized the discomfort of an especially hot summer. It was well over 100° every day for weeks and, when the afternoon sun hit the patio, the warm air collected up in the corner where the birds sat. On hot days they were soon spread out all over the roost, panting with their wings outstretched. I hung wet towels on the sides of the cage, and later I provided a small evaporative cooler to blow into the corner. This seemed to solve the problem, and they obviously enjoyed absorbing the breeze.

Finally, I was surprised to find how inept the birds were at getting about in the branches. Although naturally agile on the ground, they appeared to be awkward as tree dwellers. I added more cross members at intermediate heights, making it easier for them to get about vertically, and before long they were completely mobile again in three dimensions.

We continued to take whatever measures we could to help the birds adjust, but it was largely a matter of waiting them out.

Outside, meanwhile, the chicks were doing fine. Not the least bit reserved here, they were venturesome, playful and self-confident. They liked to zip in and out of the yucca patch and all over the lawn, inventing variations of Hawk and Quail. Flying at each other from across the way, sometimes they even attempted to involve me in their play—sitting in the middle of the yard, I might have to duck my head to avoid getting a quail in the face! Often the game had two or three of them pursuing each other through the grass—scooting in tight circles like puppies chasing each other around a bush—then hopping straight up into the air. Between times one or another would come rushing up to me or Wanda to ask for a mealworm (the pause for refreshment).

They were playful in other ways, too. One day I threw a ball of crumpled paper to them on the lawn and they played with it sporadically for the entire session. Another evening they discovered a large hummingbird moth attending to the blossoms in their favorite vinca bed. Unsure at first, they took encouragement from each other and moved in on him en masse. The moth easily avoided them, but after their third rally he appeared suddenly to lose patience and began to buzz them threateningly, one by one. Now they were not sure whether to fight or flee! After a few minutes, however, they tired of the whole thing and simply moved off to other interests, leaving the moth in charge of the flowers.

Gradually they became better about entering and leaving the new cage. Of course, like children going to bed, they always had a few important last-minute chores to delay them and to test my patience. Still, if I didn't press too hard, they responded eventually.

We hoped that our luck would continue to hold, but of course the law of probability inevitably prevailed. It came on a Monday morning, when Carrie the Cautious became "odd man out." In spite of our apprehensions, we were not prepared for it.

The birds had been racing and flying about, playing games and enjoying their outing immensely. Occasionally one flew to the top of the wall, but in a moment he would flutter safely back down to the lawn. It was all quite casual and relaxed.

Then suddenly, three of them spooked in earnest, flying rapidly across the yard and up to the hazardous, forbidden back wall. One kept on going—it was Carrie again—disappearing over the other side and down to the perilous avenue below. It was what we had dreaded all along: the unknown street and traffic.

At thirteen weeks, cautious Carrie keeps a wary eye out for danger.

The two birds on the wall came down readily at my urging, but as I peered over and called anxiously for Carrie to come back up, he merely sat at the curb, ignoring me as he studied this fascinating new area. Suddenly an automobile came speeding by, precipitating the skitterish bird off on a long, curving flight back over the neighbor's house, through the trees and out of sight toward the front.

Obviously, we had to mount a search for him, but I elected first to get the remaining four birds out of jeopardy and safely into their cage. It took a few minutes, and by then Carrie's plight looked almost hopeless—he was probably well away from his familiar territory, and there would be other passing vehicles to frighten him further.

Undismayed, the boys and I went through the neighborhood, inquiring of the neighbors but finding no clue. Finally I went to work, leaving Rob and Mike to continue looking for the missing bird.

About 4:30 they called me. The paperboy had spotted Carrie only half a block away, foraging in the pyracantha atop a neighbor's wall. Predictably, attempts at capture had found him spooky and unresponsive. I suggested they simply keep him in view until I could get there to help.

I had no more than arrived, however, when the boys appeared with Carrie in hand. He was indeed wilder than he had been and noticeably overheated. We calmed and cooled him, fed him mealworms (chicken soup), and then cautiously turned him loose in the family room. At first he kept carefully behind cover, but gradually he began to relax and soon he was calling to his fellows out on the patio. We decided to risk putting him in with them; if he made them too jumpy we could defer the evening outing.

He didn't; he adjusted so quickly that by 7 o'clock we decided to take all the birds out as usual. Carrie was not at all skittish; if anything, he was somewhat subdued, staying closer than usual to the others. The entire brood, in fact, returned to the cage in good fashion. The gamble had paid off: The situation, apparently, was back to normal.

It had been a trying, surprising day, but for the time being, at least, our incredible good fortune had held. It was to be tested again, however, in just a few days.

8

Development

We had all been relieved at Carrie's safe return. Aside from his key role in the covey, we were concerned about the little bird for his own sake. We took quite seriously our responsibility for the welfare and happiness of the five quail; we had vowed, after all, to do our best for each of them.

Outsiders, perhaps, might view our efforts to raise a brood of quail in the confines of a suburban backyard as naive or whimsical. I suppose that if we had kept the birds locked up permanently, the project might have looked more reasonable to some. We felt differently, though, and we continued to be confident in what we were doing.

Despite our concern and anxious moments, we were having fun, and we didn't have to be reminded of it any more. Taking our wards out twice a day, every day, for a half hour or more per session, was a constraining schedule (it competed with cocktail time and the evening news), but we enjoyed the outings. There was always something different and exciting; the birds took such obvious pleasure in each new adventure that it delighted us to watch. The quail were real, alive, and unpredictable—more than could be said of the summer television.

My involvement was the primary one, but Wanda joined in too, and the boys participated occasionally. Rob, whose window faced the backyard, was quick to spring to my assistance in the mornings whenever it sounded as though I needed help. In the calm of the summer evenings, he liked to lie out in the grass and let the birds swarm over him, playing King of the Hill.

Carrie, of course, had seldom had time for such lighthearted activities. Now back in the fold, he picked up promptly on his self-assigned sentry duties. The group continued to revel in new discoveries and in the expansion of their familiar territory. They began finally to show an interest in the pool area. Now they would tiptoe curiously up to its edge, standing tall and thin and peering cautiously in; then they would scurry off into the shrubs when Louie (the automatic Pool-Sweep) came chugging ponderously by.

One morning Louie coughed unexpectedly, and the birds became alarmed and flew up to the wall. After a few minutes of critical observation, they took off on a long flight, all the way back across the length of the pool, over the yucca patch and the Bermuda lawn, finally piling into their familiar corner on the opposite side of the yard. Watching them wheel off against the clear blue sky, I commented to myself that it was unrealistic to expect such a group as this to stay in a residential backyard for long.

That evening an hour or so before sunset, I called the birds out of the cage as usual. In their exuberance they took to the air immediately at the edge of the patio, flying past me on their way to the corner flower bed. Suddenly there was another crisis.

As they flew around the corner, Brownie spotted trouble first and doubled back in midflight, heading off to the right, over the pool to the opposite wall, where they all had been that morning. The others, however, were less observant and continued to their familiar flower bed. Here they found themselves landing practically atop Blacky, the neighbors' cat, who had suddenly materialized in the junipers. Just as the birds were setting down, the opportunistic feline made a pounce at them, sending Carrie up over the back wall, Pearl down into the side yard, and Rose and Red-Leg back to the cage. Now he was after Pearl and, in hurrying to her defense, I inadvertently frightened her off toward the front, into the same general area where Carrie had impacted earlier in the week.

It was another hectic, excited moment; the flurry brought the whole family. I managed to recover Brownie, and we closed him into the cage with Rose and Red-Leg. Meanwhile Blacky had retreated over the wall, but we found such a pile of feathers that we speculated briefly on whether he had actually caught one of the birds. There was no other evidence, however, and, consulting together, we concluded that the missing two had gone out of sight in opposite directions—Carrie over the back wall, across the road, and out into the vacant lots; Pearl out front, across the street, and into a group of contiguous backyards.

We activated our Search and Inquiry Plan, but dusk was falling rapidly and we held little hope. As the sun settled behind the mountains, we walked around the quiet neighborhood calling "Chuk-CAW, Chuck-CAW-caw!" (What did the passing pedestrian make of us?) The boys scouted the extremities in both directions but without success.

Then, just as the sun was gone and we were regrouping on the patio, suddenly there came a half-grown quail whirring unexpectedly across the road like some feathery, airborne egg beater, lighting first on the neighbor's back wall, and then flying on up to the roof! It was Carrie, of course, and soon he was exchanging calls with the others in the cage. We called him over readily, and once he had found our familiar stretch of wall he was on his way home.

Remarking again upon our continued good fortune, we looked up just in time to see Pearl making a similar approach from the opposite direction, over the other neighbor's roof. It was dusk now and slower going, but before it was completely dark she too had found the cage.

We could scarcely believe our uncanny luck. As night fell, here again was the whole unlikely brood safe and sound behind the wire mesh, charming and nonchalant as they perched comfortably upon their favorite mesquite roost. Before going to bed (and several times during the night), I looked out to check on them. There they were, settled and serene and innocent as ever—one, two, three, four, five ridiculous little birds, all in a row. Somehow, it *still* seemed like the right number.

Airborne from the patio roof to the lava rock below.

The next morning, a Friday, I took the quail out for a full hour. They were impeccably behaved; cautious perhaps, even self-conscious, but with no disposition to scatter. Together we investigated the less well-known grounds—around the pool, the planter, and the other side of the yucca patch, preparing ourselves for the next crisis. The birds stayed close together and kept a sharp eye on me, apparently looking for guidance. When we returned finally to the more familiar Bermuda lawn and flower beds, they spread out again and relaxed, safe at home once more.

That weekend we had more long outings, exploring all over the area. At the quails' initiative, we went into the kitchen and the family room for lengthy sessions. It almost seemed that they understood and shared our plan to push for familiarity with a greater "home territory." It occurred to us, too, that each instance of their flying away, followed by safe return, probably served to fix their territorial connection all the more.

For a time things remained relatively quiet, and our program of exploration continued into the twelfth week. On Sunday evening, Red-Leg led the way into the palm fronds along the back wall; the rest positioned themselves among them and chirped delightedly at each other. Next morning they took over the north neighbor's wall, exploring it at length, and in the evening they repeated the exercise to the south. This time, however, Carrie was jumpy and Red-Leg elected to cut the session short, taking the entire group back to the cage (perhaps Blacky was lurking about).

The birds began to fly even more in getting from place to place, and before long they were going into the palms and the olive tree regularly, and sometimes up to the roof. Spooky Quail became wilder and more exuberant, and occasionally we found ourselves caught up in the midst of it, ducking and flinching as the birds made passes at us. It was a rousing game as they came bouncing up into the air or streaking out of the yucca, flapping and skidding along the deck, punctuating their excitement with peeps and chirps.

In the midst of all this activity the quail were experiencing a new spurt of growth. It showed first in their legs and feet, and their new tail feathers were nearly an inch longer than those they replaced. Ironically, the effect of longer legs and tails (until the rest of their bodies could catch up) was to make the birds resemble their archenemies, the hawks or vultures.

With regard to overall size, individuals varied from time to time. At the moment Brownie was slightly the largest and Pearl the smallest, but there was very little actual difference between them. Pearl seemed to me to be generally dainty and demure (but I was looking closely for distinctive male markings anywhere I might find them!). By this time all *five* had developed the colorful side feathers, and hence were less distinguishable from each other than ever. Red-Leg had a line where his cap should begin and Carrie had a similar slight indication, but, for the most part, they were practically identical. In the matter of gender, I was still frankly baffled.

While their markings remained essentially the same, their personalities were diverging and it was intriguing to follow their development. Red-Leg continued to emerge as the nominal leader of the group, his original identification as youngster and outlander all but forgotten. It occurred to me that perhaps his initial detachment, manifesting itself as apparent independence or self-assurance, was what had led the others to view him intuitively as mature and hence as a source of guidance. He was still less susceptible to group pressures and, when engaged in an interesting activity of his own, was likely to ignore the others and their momentary enthusiasms. Nor was he particularly inclined to respond to our human requests or to solicit treats from us. It seemed that he related to us strictly on a pragmatic basis, without the emotional dependence.

Interestingly, I sometimes felt that I was competing with Red-Leg for control of the group. In particular, when I attempted to call the birds back into the cage, his behavior often seemed to be the key—if he entered willingly the others were quick to follow, but if he hung back they stayed out too. It was as though they needed his approval to return.

In considering this, I felt a little put down at first. Here I was, after all, a member of *the* intelligent species of the planet, with nearly a half-century of life experience to draw upon, matching wits (not too successfully) with a tiny, adolescent bundle of feathers not even three months out of his shell! Reflecting further, however, I began to be amused at the idea. Then I felt pleased, and finally I was somehow vaguely reassured. Sometime later, I decided, I would have to think about that.

A young pine tree in the backyard provides a deceptively natural setting.

9

Homestretch

September arrived in Las Vegas; the boys returned to school, but summer lingered on—clear, calm, and beautiful. The quail, now into their thirteenth week, were settled, too, and comfortable. I decided to take another step toward our objective of free birds in an open cage.

Not that the birds appeared to resent their confinement—they seldom paced about as zoo animals do, looking for a way out. When it was time for an outing, my appearance at their aviary might set off a little flurry of anticipatory activity; otherwise they seemed quite content in their wire-mesh home. Actually, they may have considered themselves free already. Indeed, they practically were—there were extended periods at least twice a day when they could go wherever they chose and return pretty much on their own terms.

It was this aspect of their situation that I wished to encourage. It would be ideal, we thought, if the birds could leave the cage or reenter it at their convenience, even when we were not at home. Perhaps this would not prove possible, but I wanted to try.

We recognized that it was no simple matter to have the cage at once both open and yet secure. Obviously, for example, I could not just remove the large front panel, leaving the birds exposed. Near the top, however, there were some interesting small openings, niches under the eaves; I felt that if the birds could learn to utilize these properly, they might be left open with relative safety. It would be difficult for a cat, say, to negotiate them, and anyway, the slightest activity on the sheet aluminum roof would surely

53

provide a warning racket (I was underestimating our shrewd neighbor, Blacky).

To try out the scheme, I selected a convenient niche, and at exercise time I removed the mesh from it. I tried to coax the quail through the opening, and, as usual, they seemed to understand what I wanted. Despite their considerable interest, though, they would not come out. I suppose to them it looked awkward and hazardous, and so they just dropped down to exit as usual through the familiar front panel at floor level.

After several such unsuccessful attempts, I installed at the niche a bow-shaped piece of driftwood, leading over the top of the cage. Cantilevered in both directions, it formed a sort of stile from their upper roosts over to the outside. Apparently it was just what was needed, for now they found it great fun to hop over to this natural catwalk and step on out. They walked to and fro on it, testing it out with obvious delight, occasionally pausing to perch on the end and peer down buzzardlike at the patio below. Even so, it was another day before any would venture to use it as an actual access-way to their outing, and then they would not fly directly down to the patio but hopped first to the roof, where they could walk cautiously out to the front edge and flutter down to the familiar yucca patch below.

I had not intended such elaboration, but it would do for a start, and before long they were all doing this much, at least. Still, when it came time to return they preferred for some time to use the large, lower-level access panel, and only occasionally would they fly back up to reenter through the niche and stile.

With a trap-door and a "stile" to the eaves, the new aviary gives the quail plenty of interesting accessways and viewpoints.

I was unwilling yet to risk leaving the new exit permanently open, so I mounted the mesh cover on hinges and ran a drawstring down the wall, enabling me to open and close it remotely. At exercise time I pulled open this trapdoor and encouraged the birds to exit via the interesting new route. They responded eagerly, and after a while they began to return this way occasionally, too. I had to keep the lower panel open as an alternative, though, for if I *required* them to come back through the new stile, they might get confused, and one or another was sure to become hopelessly lost in the eaves. A particularly unproductive flurry and clamor would result then, with the birds on the *outside* calling for help and scurrying into all the wrong places, while the birds on the *inside* alternately scolded or encouraged them or demonstrated (usually incorrectly) the proper path for reentry. I was learning to be patient, however, and I simply stood by while they worked things out at their own pace.

Meanwhile, I was pleased to see how relaxed they had become in the yard. They were less likely to fly off at unexpected noises and, when they did, it was only for a brief escapade. As usual, Red-Leg and Carrie served the important function of setting the limits of behavior for the group. A jotting in my journal at this time reads:

> Red-Leg's role as leader of the family continues to evolve. In the cage, he spends much of his time relaxing on the uppermost roost, casually overseeing the domain, but dozing frequently, and relying upon Carrie the Cautious (one level below) to keep a sharp eye out. Although the others appear somewhat deferential toward him, he does not behave in an ill-tempered or domineering way. Thus far, in fact, we have observed no bullying or intimidation among the group at all, or any further head-pecking incidents (like the one when little Red-Leg persuaded the others to settle down and roost for the night). Occasionally, however, as the leader he does appear to assume some responsibility for the others—going back for a straggler or calling for Pearl to come down from the roof.

> From our point of view, Red-Leg is a good choice, for his judgment is often surprisingly astute. In the various crises and alarums, he has seldom flown into a windowpane or to a precarious location; he is more liable to fly back to the safety of the cage. His self-assurance appears to have a moderating effect upon the others too, perhaps balancing out Carrie's tendency to overreact. In a scatter situation, while Carrie flies off, Red-Leg remains cool, and the other three are likely to choose a reaction somewhere in between.

We, too, were learning to keep calm during these skirmishes, concluding that no one but Carrie was likely to go beyond our yard. Furthermore, if we could stay unconcerned, we were sure he would come whirring back in a few minutes.

Inevitably, I suppose, with so much contact, we began to get some feeling of special communication with the individual birds. Initially it was little more than a flash of mutual recognition or a moment of complementary behavior. I saw it first when Pearl marched up and stood eye to eye with me to ask for a treat and when Carrie sulked, after we had captured him to freshen his markings (we still needed these to follow individual behavior).

We were looking for such indications, of course, for in our previous experience we had eventually established a remarkably close rapport with Peep-Sight. He, however, had been taken into our home and family right at the start and the relationship had grown over several years, whereas these birds, only a few months old, had had contact mainly with each other and only secondarily with us. Significantly, they still saw themselves as quail, I think, and us as people (unlike their predecessor, who apparently merged the two).

While their personalities were shifting and developing, the relative size of the birds changed constantly too—it depended upon which day you looked at them! In any case, they all appeared well fed, presumably finding sufficient variety for balanced intake and healthy growth. They had added a few new foods to their diet, discovering cheese, peanuts, and even cottage cheese when their exercise time overlapped into our cocktail hour. From the morning sessions, they had determined that bacon, papaya, cantaloupe, grapefruit, and Cocoa Puffs were edibles. Nor did the eventual popularity of cherry breakfast rolls surprise us, for the delights of cherry pie filling were well known to all. Unlike Peep-Sight, however, they showed no interest in fruit juice or soft drinks.

Along with size, personality, and appetite, the quail were changing in outward appearance as well. Soon they all began to moult heavily, particularly on their heads, where plume and face feathers were replaced at a rapid rate. It was clear that they were approaching maturity; every day they looked different to us.

Then, midway through the thirteenth week, almost overnight they made a breathtaking transformation, both in manner and appearance. Instead of scurrying about like rodents, suddenly they moved with grace and poise. Their proportions were nearly back in balance and their plumage had taken on a sleek and sculptured look. They were self-assured and most imposing, whether fluffed out for effect or simply standing straight and thin, like pickets on a fence.

When foraging, the group began sometimes to move off on its own, around the corner of the house and out of view, satisfied to keep in touch with an occasional "Chuk-CAW." Sparrows on the lawn were driven off quickly, and the formerly feared mockingbird, touching down at the other side of the pool, was taken aback to look up and see this delegation of gray-frocked bowling pins wheeling smoothly across the deck to demand the nature of his business. Their confidence was infectious, and we all felt more relaxed.

Despite their surge to maturity, however, there remained that one unresolved question—that nagging, frustrating area of confusion and bewilderment: which of them was a rooster and which was a hen? The differences were long overdue, but where were the distinctive male markings?

Not knowing what else to do, the poker player in me decided to stand on my original bet: i.e., that the five of them constituted a Full House—three of one kind 'and a pair of the other. Meanwhile, in a somewhat plaintive notation at the bottom of a page, the semiscientist scrawled in his chronicle:

Now the tiny head feathers are coming in rapidly—these will form the masks and caps. The patterns are indistinct, but soon they will tell the tale, probably by tomorrow. Finally, *then*, we will know the truth. And *finally*, we will see what kind of predictor I am.

Nearly full grown, the quail will soon fit its feathers.

10

Showdown

As it turned out, if Jimmy the Greek was worried, he could relax—he had nothing to fear from me. When it came to making predictions, I'd surely have done as well by simply flipping a coin, or five coins. At any rate, what should have been obvious all along, I suppose (and may have been to the reader) had finally become so to us.

It was exquisitely logical: the reason we had failed to observe any gender-related color variations was quite simply because there were none—the chicks were all of the same sex. Furthermore, the absence of male markings—russet caps, black masks and bibs—was entirely appropriate, for all the birds were *females*.

There could be no doubt of it now; by mid-September the quail were practically full-grown and, completing their moult into adult plumage, they showed the full contours of mature birds. They were handsome and colorful but, look as one might, there was not a russet cap or a black mask to be seen anywhere among them. I had to face it: what I thought was a Full House had turned out to be Five of a Kind.

Somewhat embarrassed, I wondered how we could have deceived ourselves for so long. It had been possible only in the total absence of males. With even one rooster, we should surely have seen the truth much sooner. In any case but this, in fact, there would have been definite markings in the sixth or seventh week, just as we had expected. The likelihood of no cocks at all was so remote (with five chicks the statistical probability is about one chance in 32) that it was little wonder we had hardly considered it se-

59

riously. Instead, we had imagined that we saw the beginnings of the male markings first in one bird and then another. It had been easy, since hens do show a suggestion of them, too.

But be that as it may, the fact was that what we *had* was five young females. We were disappointed, but then we remembered that our primary goal had always been to raise as many of the chicks as possible to healthy adult status. We could not complain about our success and good fortune on that count—all five had made it. I suspect the statistical probability here, too, was no more than a few percent. We could be proud of what our efforts and concern had achieved.

Even so, it was difficult to change our thinking. We had to realize, for example, that we were not going to find a potentially mateable pair in *this* group—that aspect of our plan, at least, would have to be abandoned. It was particularly difficult, too, to reverse our early and long-standing identification of Red-Leg (our "wild-card") as a male. It seemed as though she had some trouble accepting the revelation herself, for she became quite irritable for a day or two, pecking the others and bullying them for no apparent reason. (Perhaps she was disappointed to find herself consigned thus to an all-female society and simply expressed her chagrin in the time-honored tradition, i.e., with inappropriately directed aggression!)

Reflecting upon the events of the summer, we were struck again with the parallels that it had afforded to the raising of our own children. First there had been that initial helplessness and dependence, the early efforts at learning, the rapid acquisition of new capabilities; then eventually the awkwardness of adolescence and the ambivalent striving for independence; finally (thank goodness), the welcome beginnings of good judgment and mature viewpoint. In the case of the quail, the whole cycle had been compressed into three and a half months—often we had been able to solve problems with temporary measures, for they would be outgrown in a few days anyway. Too bad, we thought, that one couldn't do the same with human children. In either case, however, the responsible "parent" must always be alert to risks and perils and accept his share of the responsibility.

The analogy was good, but the pace had left us a little exhausted. We had invested considerable effort and attention in bringing our adopted family this far. For us these fourteen weeks had been an exciting mixture of adventure and anxiety, of frustration and success; it had been fun, all right, but tiring. Now we were ready for calmer days, ready to relax and contemplate a job well done, ready to enjoy our grown children as friends (and to forget our distracting preoccupation with their welfare).

But the Gambel's quail take fifteen weeks to mature fully, and we had one more week to go. As it began, we found that we were in for a few anxious moments yet, and still further tests of the celebrated stamina of the species.

Sunday started early. A racket on the patio brought me scrambling out of bed to drive off Blacky, who had stopped by on the way home from his customary Saturday night's revelry to make a token charge at the girls. No damage done, but they had been badly frightened and were jamming up into

Checking on Blacky, the neighborhood cat, from the safety of the wall.

awkward places. Although he was still offhand in his approach, it was becoming clear that Blacky's interest was not to be dismissed too lightly.

The birds recovered quickly, but to make up for their hectic night we invited them to remain outside with us for most of the next day. It was a golden September Sunday, and we were all lazy and comfortable in the backyard. The girls loved it. They ranged about freely, playing Spooky Quail on the patio, flying up to the walls and roof and occasionally into the neighbors' trees. From time to time they came to scratch and peck at the newspaper or to pull at my shoe laces or scavenge in the ashes of last night's barbecue. Periodically they would chase the sparrows off the lawn. Pearl boldly flew up to the roof to send the mockingbird packing, and all five scolded him in absentia for several minutes thereafter.

Then at a loud noise they suddenly took flight, and Rose smashed into the dining room window. The large pane undulated but somehow remained intact; Rose, however, was stunned. After a few moments we saw that it was worse than we had thought—the impact had jammed her upper bill back into her head; the lower one, still undamaged, jutted out grotesquely underneath. The poor bewildered thing could only make rasping sounds through her apparently broken face.

We felt terrible, wondering what we might have to do, but we decided to let her recover her bearings before examining her more carefully. While we watched anxiously, Rose shook herself, sneezed several times, and then, incredibly, her beak snapped back out into its proper position! It was unimpaired after all, not even a crack—apparently it was sufficiently pliable to telescope inward at the impact, bending at her nostrils without fracturing. We were immensely relieved, even though we knew there might yet be delayed effects. A few weeks later she did lose a patch of tiny head feathers, but except for this temporary baldness she apparently had survived the collision successfully. She was good as ever from then on.

Once more we had enjoyed astonishing good fortune, but there were still more crises to come. In the afternoon, relaxing again, I heard a tremendous thud and, hurrying over to the patio, I found Brownie beneath the kitchen window (again, somehow intact), flopping about in small circles, unable to stand. She managed shortly to recover her balance, but this time, while there was no problem with her beak, there was certainly injury involved. For some time the poor bird could only stand quietly, eyes closed, a tragic little figure.

Brownie remained thus, stunned and dopey, for several days. She tried to stay with the others, but tired quickly outside and preferred to spend her time dozing. She would not attempt to fly, and when she walked, holding her head so close in to her shoulders, she was unable to move it for normal balance. It was touching to see her bobbing painfully along like some funny, odd shore bird. From her movements, we suspected that she had broken one or more bones.

For a week or so Brownie continued to look stiff and sore, and we feared that she was permanently crippled. When she tried to fly up to the bird bath or to the palm tree, she fell pathetically short. She learned to compensate for her weaknesses in various ways, though, and by the end of the next week she could fly awkwardly up to the roosts or down from the patio roof, simply by aiming beyond her target. We gave her special attention, of course, and we were gratified when she began gradually to improve. Soon she was even participating (though not too effectively) in Hawk and Quail.

Slowly she continued to recover. One day, when Red-Leg slipped squawking into the pool and sent everyone flying off in alarm, Brownie found in the ensuing excitement that she could easily make it to the top of the wall. This appeared to be a milestone. Evidently there were no broken bones after all, and she had clearly regained her strength and spirit. Soon it was obvious: Brownie was back! It was a gratifying and inspiring recuperation. Once again the birds had amazed us with their tremendous capacity to survive and endure.

Now we felt that we could confirm that fifteen weeks was a proper estimate for the growing period of Gambel's quail—ours were finally settled and mature. Their proportions were nicely in balance, and, except for Brownie (whose neck motion remained slightly limited for some time), all were graceful and efficient in their movements. Occasionally, they still enjoyed a childish game of Spooky Quail, but what we had at this point were five fine young adults.

As things returned to normal, I noticed that the birds frequently returned to their cage via the trap door, easily finding the proper niche. Encouraged, I proceeded to construct a second door on the diagonally opposite corner. This time they seemed to know immediately what I was doing, and they were clamoring to try it out long before I was ready. When finally it was done, they were delighted to find that it enabled them to exit from their cage through one niche, walk up across the roof and back in through the other, then back out again! It was such a happy discovery that they went round and round repeatedly, enjoying their new freedom and chattering excitedly.

October came and went and our days passed pleasantly as the hot weather finally moderated. The girls had definitely settled into a mature stability; there was little arguing or head-pecking, and they remained well within the geographic limits we had hoped to establish for them. They liked to march officiously back and forth on top of the walls, gossiping or commenting self-righteously about what they saw on the other side, but they seldom ventured over. Spooky Quail became an infrequent activity, and the episodes of window-bumping diminished sharply. It was interesting, when one of them did have such an accident, to see that Red-Leg would approach the dazed bird and try to distract her from her pain by assuming the invitational position of the playful puppy! Generally the girls had become quite enjoyable and manageable, and we were all relaxed together.

Despite the stability of the situation, we still had no definite idea as to what disposition we would ultimately make of the birds. Would we have house quail or not, and which ones would they be? As the weeks went by, we began to evolve a plan. We recalled that the coveys would begin collecting at common feeding grounds in late January or February; they would form then into the winter "super flocks" in the area near Newton's Corners. This would be the time for matchmaking, we thought, for new pairings for the spring season soon to come. And this would be the time, if we chose, to take Carrie, Red-Leg and Brownie, for example, out to the desert and release them. If we could bring ourselves to do it, we felt quite sure that this trio could make its own way. Rose and Pearl, then, would remain to become our house quail, consistent with their apparent inclination. The two females would surely get along well and provide each other company. Perhaps we could dismantle the cage and let them live inside with us as Peep-Sight had done, to become, after all, a part of the family.

It seemed a potentially workable idea and rather appealing. The hardest part, of course, would be in turning out Brownie, Carrie, and Red-Leg. Could we satisfy ourselves that in the long run this would be for the best? We had become so fond of all five that it would require our collective determination to separate them.

Still, it was only a tentative plan. We had several months to think about it. When the time came, we would see how we felt—we could, indeed, "let spontaneity and intuition have their day." For now, we said, let's finally just relax. Perhaps, at last, we have earned the right to sit back, draw a calm breath, and enjoy the company of our grown "children."

11

The Girls at Home

Happily, we found that we had in fact arrived at a phase which was considerably less hectic than the previous one. There were few crises now—the mature quail were relatively even of temperament and hence more predictable. Their numerous exploits of the summer and early autumn had apparently provided them exactly the experience necessary to learn about survival in the conglomerated patchwork of city and desert that was Las Vegas. True, there were still hazards and surprises awaiting us, but we contemplated these with the confidence of seasoned veterans. Perhaps a certain self-assurance was finally justified.

As fully grown adults, the quail were truly beautiful: well-proportioned, glistening with health, and pleasing to the eye. Furthermore, they looked perfectly natural in our backyard setting. Of course, we should still have preferred to see at least one black-masked face somewhere among them, but we found continuing satisfaction, nonetheless, just in being with them. They obviously disliked being held and so we restrained ourselves; but on our outings they were likely to jump up to a shoulder or crawl about upon us, and this generally satisfied our natural urge to pet them.

As the quail had grown, our routine outside had evolved and adjusted, too, and it differed now from what it had been. For one thing, with the days becoming shorter it was dark by the time I reached home after work, and the birds had already retired to their roosts. We rescheduled the second outing to my lunch hour. This was usually a comfortable time of day, and the quiet outdoor interlude provided a nice break in my office routine.

I'd fix a quick sandwich to eat outside, and the "girls" (now poised young ladies) would head immediately for a sunny flower bed to begin their daily dust bath. Getting right at it, they were able to perform their ablutions and be out shaking themselves clean in only fifteen or twenty minutes. After a moment of sunning, they were ready to return directly to the cage. I rewarded them then with two or three mealworms apiece, and they'd settle in on the upper roosts for a siesta. The noon session became a well-knit exercise, and my wards seldom made me tardy in returning to work.

The morning sessions had changed, too, and included the side yards. The birds liked to get out as soon as it was light, and I liked having them back before the neighborhood got too busy. The result was that we all favored an early start. With the sun rising later, it was still chilly when we stepped out into our westward-facing backyard, and so in making our rounds we took a somewhat brisker pace.

The first place the sun's rays reached was the south side, and the girls liked to begin here, exploring the woodpile. Aside from its location in the early sunshine, this structure was fascinating to them in its own right, too. The sticks of firewood were piled loosely together, leaving quail-sized openings throughout, and the whole stack was set out from the wall about six inches—there was plenty of room behind to turn around. The birds never tired of investigating this maze; they checked it out every day. Their great delight was in darting in and out and changing levels; in the process, they'd peck at insects and bits of bark or fiber and exchange comments from adjacent corridors. I had to laugh when all five were energetically exploring this honeycomb, popping in one hole and out another: It looked like a typical sequence from the old Keystone Comedies.

As winter progressed, the woodpile shrank, and I found myself selecting the evening's supply of firewood from among the pieces which would least effect the integrity of the girls' playhouse. Even so, they noticed every reduction in it, and whenever we had had an especially cozy evening in the family room they were sure to remark upon it the next day, noting the missing sticks.

In due course I ordered a new supply of wood. The birds were so overwhelmed by this sudden addition that for three days they wouldn't go into the stack at all! Instead, they stood looking up at it in awe, commenting to each other upon this remarkable replenishment. Finally its attraction was just too much for them, and they plunged back inside again, performing their Mack Sennett antics with renewed enthusiasm.

After a while the quail would tire of the woodpile, and one of them might look up and notice the neighbor's apple tree reaching over to our side, just above the wall. Then she would probably fly up to perch in its boughs and peck at the buds and twigs, and soon all five would be on top of the wall, parading to and fro and scolding the neighbor's pets in self-righteous chorus.

Often the next step would be a sudden explosive take-off on one of their long flights—joyful and rowdy as they "shotgunned" all the way around to the opposite side of the yard. Or, in a calmer mood, they might elect simply to fly quietly down to graze on the Bermuda and alyssum or to test the nearly ripe pyracantha berries. Perhaps they would fly up to the birdbath for a drink or scoop up the droplets of water the sprinklers had left behind on the iris leaves. Eventually then I would lead them around the pool to the other side yard to inspect another whole set of favorite rocks and shrubs. Any change here from the previous sessions was sure to draw comment, too. A new bag of fertilizer leaning unobtrusively against the wall was cause for concern, and when a second one showed up the following day their suspicions were reinforced.

Ultimately the top of this wall was patrolled, too, and again, the birds might elect to launch off it en masse on a raucous return flight. I was pleased when they took to the air several times per outing, for I thought that the exercise was good for them. Sometimes, however, we just continued our walk—around the planters, back to the yucca patch and then to the patio— returning to the cage and breakfast.

On the weekends we had more time, and so we took the quail out for longer periods, several times a day. They appeared to recognize that things were different: There was no routine. Often Wanda and I would relax with some interest of our own and let the girls range randomly about the entire yard. Sometimes we just watched.

One could still note individual variations in the appearance and demeanor of the mature birds, but there had been some merging of features as well. Rose and Pearl performed occasionally as sentry now, and Red-Leg had become both more people-oriented and part of the group. In size, there was practically no difference at all once they were full-grown. Brownie's formerly stiff neck was happily back to normal, and Rose had regrown the small patch of feathers that she had lost off the top of her head when she had collided with the window.

Differences among the adult birds were especially evident in their vocal patterns, and I noted these in my journal. It took several months of checking and listening to sort them out, but eventually I was able to identify and characterize the special "signature" of each of the five individuals. My final summary on the subject read as follows:

> Having listened carefully now to many calling quail, including, of course, our own, I am persuaded that there is a basic or standard call of the Gambel's, which consists of a three-word structure, generally repeated two or more times. This fundamental phrase sounds to me like "Chuk-CAW-caw!"
>
> The first two "words" are of only one syllable each—the initial one being quite staccato and "down," while the second word is loud and emphatic, generally rising and drawn out. Individual differences appear in these words, but mostly in pitch and timbre. The third word, however, is subject to greater variation, including even omission. (Peep-Sight typically employed it only in his final repetition: "Chuk-CAW, Chuk-CAW, Chuk-CAW-caw!")
>
> Brownie's call, I note, is close to this standard phrasing, "Chuk-CAW-caw!" as is Rose's, but the latter's is pitched several tones higher, giving it a special, recog-

The author encourages investigation of the rapidly diminishing woodpile. The birdbath is another favorite spot. (Photos by Robert Plummer)

nizable urgency. Carrie and Pearl use the standard beginning and regular pitch, but then each employs a third word which has *two* syllables. Carrie's has only a suggestion of separation: "Chuk-CAW-caw-uh!" while Pearl's is quite pronounced: "Chuk-CAW-*chigga!*"

The calls of the four true sisters show a close family resemblance, but as usual, the maverick Red-Leg incorporates completely distinctive features all her own. Her call is structurally like Pearl's, but she delivers it with a totally different and unusual emphasis, hitting all three words with equal strength: "CHUK-CAW-CHIGGA!" It is an unmistakable and, in my experience, uncommon call, individually recognizable.

When loud and well projected, the calls are readily distinguishable, but at other times, as when grazing, the birds call softly, almost in a whisper, without opening their beaks at all. Indeed, they appear able to modulate the effective range of their calls according to the needs of the moment, all the way from the full-throated clarion cry, audible a block or more away, down to the *sotto voce* of muted conversations in the yucca patch. In the latter case the features are muffled, and it is hard to recognize whose call it is or where it originates.

From time to time, while the birds were growing up I had attempted to master the calls myself. Self-conscious at first, I eventually gained confidence, and the birds called back, encouraging me.

One day I had occasion to check out my skill. Coming home after work I found that Wanda and Rob had taken the girls out for an extra session and got caught off guard. Just as darkness fell, two of the birds had flown off across the back wall and out of sight into an unfamiliar yard. Taking his flashlight, Rob had found one of them (Brownie) perched in a bush, and managed to recover her, but the other (courageous Carrie) was still out there somewhere, stuck on a roof or tree. There was so much traffic and activity that we agreed it would be best just to let her keep her own security for the night—after all, she'd had plenty of practice at hiding out in strange places! We hoped she would wait and pick the proper time in the morning to return.

Of course, as soon as the sun came up I was outside at the back wall, calling "Chuk-CAW, Chuk-CAW!" out into the quiet neighborhood. Behind me the four quail in the cage took up the chorus, but Carrie didn't reply. Then in a short while, here she came unannounced, whirring over the side wall from the north. Apparently while we were calling she had casually worked her way back to the adjacent yard, where she could assure herself that all was well. At any rate, Carrie was back, and my confidence, in some obscure way, seemed to have been vindicated.

As calls developed and our relationships stabilized, fall turned to winter. With December came the first hard freeze, and one morning on their outing the girls were surprised to discover that the iris were not sprinkled with the usual droplets, but with solid beads of ice instead. Upon investigating, they found these crunchy "seeds" of water to be a happy innovation (comparable in importance, no doubt, to the invention of the Popsicle). A little later the birds flew up to the birdbath, where they were further astounded to find themselves standing on *top* of the water, rather than with their feet comfortably immersed in it. This time they were disappointed to learn that this "hard" water couldn't be scooped up in their beaks.

They turned away then and began walking around the pool, where they came upon yet another amazing transformation. Overnight, the little pomegranate tree had shed all its leaves and now stood bare and exposed in the chilly air, like September Morn. The boys had long since harvested its abundant fruit, but the foliage clung and the shrub had always seemed too dense for the birds to enter. Suddenly today it was an open and attractive perch. The girls remarked upon this puzzling phenomenon at length; then, as though of one mind, they all flew up to hop awkwardly about in the maze of fine branches, enjoying their new-found perspective on a familiar corner of the yard.

Once the birds were back in the cage, Wanda wondered aloud whether they would have trouble adapting to the freezing temperatures that could be expected now at night. After all, it had been consistently over 100° only a few weeks before! Of course, the quail were indigenous to the area and presumably adaptable to its weather, but still, the confines of the cage might somehow impair their ability to do so. Thinking she might be right, I installed fiberglass insulation in the roosting cove up under the eaves, and then I looped nine feet of heating cable around its periphery and under the boughs. It was only 45-watts of warmth, but it should be roughly equivalent to another five quail, I thought, and about right for moderating the cold December nights. The cable turned on automatically at 38°, and soon we were noticing its neon indicator flickering early each evening, as our nighttime temperatures approached the low 30s.

The comfortable cage was becoming a complex installation, what with its trapdoors, its potted plants, and its temperature-sensitive heating. And there was to be even more. Of course, as I introduced each new feature I had to proceed carefully, acquainting the girls with it, bit by bit. The roll-up blinds on each side of the cage, for example, were a great protection against the wind and provided some concealment, but the birds viewed them with characteristic suspicion. Even though installed in the dark of night, and rolled down only an inch or two each day, it had been touch and go. Slowly and with patience, that was the way to success.

Yes, we were learning. It was funny—when Peep-Sight first came to us in May of 1969, we knew that we were ignorant in the ways of Gambel's quail. After four years with him, we thought that we had learned enough to be somewhat authoritative on the species. We presumed occasionally to answer questions and even to provide advice to others. Now, however, after spending the summer of '74 observing in detail the intricate behavioral development of Carrie, Red-Leg, Brownie, Rose, and Pearl, we could only *begin* to appreciate how much there was to learn and how far we had yet to go. And what a fascinating prospect it was.

12

Lessons in Review

While a part of what we were learning about the birds was new to us, other aspects of their behavior appeared to reconfirm our previous findings. Sometimes what we saw led us instead to revise earlier beliefs. Of course there were too few data and too many uncontrolled variables to be certain of any general conclusions, but still we enjoyed observing the differences and similarities and comparing the behavior of these quail with that of the estimable Peep-Sight. Our approach was only semiscientific, but it was fun, and we thought that it had value.

Insofar as comparisons with Peep-Sight were concerned, we had first to acknowledge, of course, that there were important basic differences. Primarily, there was the matter of gender; but beyond this, the two situations were quite dissimilar. Peep-Sight had lived in the house as part of our family, with no other creatures than ourselves to relate to. He was with us constantly. Somehow he had reconciled his instincts to those special circumstances, and we had all enjoyed the consequences of his remarkable adaptation. Our present birds, however, lived together outside in a "home" of their own and spent only a few hours each day in our company. They saw us frequently, but they were their own constant companions. Unlike Peep-Sight, they were not members of our family; yet, for an hour or two each day, perhaps some of us were members of theirs. How then, did *they* perceive the world, and us?

When I was with them, certainly I was in some respects their parent or guardian, and at times my presence must have been critical. They had reached a point where all five would dust bathe together if I sat close by—even Carrie would relinquish her duties then (albeit reluctantly) to enjoy a rare, off-duty respite as I stood guard. I was surprised, too, to notice that the birds appeared to be more willing to feed when I was at hand, just as Peep-Sight had been. In the cage at eating time, one or another might take up a post atop the seed dispenser, but they still preferred having me (or Wanda) visible through the kitchen windows. Also, although they would come out of the trapdoors readily and onto the patio roof, for a while they would not fly down to the lava rock below unless I was there to coax them. (Eventually, any one of us in view would do, and in time they learned to make the move independently.) Finally, if I walked out past their cage and out of sight, they were likely to call after me until I returned. Wanda reported, too, that when she took them out in my absence, they sometimes called out off-handedly while they foraged, as though inviting me to come and join them.

Nonetheless, despite my special role, these birds did not seem heavily dependent upon human association; I don't believe that we were an essential part of their world. In many ways they were sufficient unto themselves; they looked after each other. Occasionally, for example, they appeared to groom each other in a special fashion. When one had a broken feather, or a bit of dirt in an awkward place, another was likely to help out with a tug or a peck. This did not seem to be a punitive or aggressive move, but rather it seemed an expression of sisterly interest in the other's appearance. ("Here, dear, let me get that lint off your skirt.")

In watching the quail interact so closely and seeing how readily they learned, I began to wonder whether it was possible that the lessons of one could somehow be transmitted to the others. Could one who had already fallen into the pool, or flown into a window, help another avoid making the same error? Maybe it was simply a matter of warning the other away at the proper time, until eventually the inexperienced one became conditioned to the same hazard without actually having suffered the attendant "hard knocks." It was an interesting possibility that my intuition continued to favor, but there was no evidence in my journal to support it. Indeed, I found that during the course of growing up *each* of the five had slipped squawking into the pool just once and that *every one* had personally tested the deceitful windowpanes. Of course there were other, undocumented areas of their learning, where some such Pavlovian principle may have been involved—the idea may be worthy of further examination.

In any case, it was great fun to see the birds learn and develop, while trying not to interfere unduly in their lives. As I watched, I tried also to keep a receptive mind, and to the extent that I succeeded sometimes I was rewarded with a surprise. A notable example was the reversal of my view of the Gambel's as being generally inept in the air.

Quail are basically ground birds, after all, and one's natural assumption therefore is that they are awkward and limited in flight. With such a predisposition, it is easy to see supporting evidence. On the ground, for example, we know that they weave and career about like animated roller skates, but when they take to the air, we see them in the apparent confusion of noisy, scattering flight. Casually viewed, they appear as inefficient, unskilled flyers. Perhaps this impression is useful in misleading their enemies, but in my opinion the quail are capable of remarkable agility in flight.

My reeducation on this point started when I observed the girls making sharp turns or sudden stops in midair. As usual, they were especially adept in familiar surroundings—they were able to maneuver rapidly into or through the roosts and even to reverse in midflight when encountering some unexpected obstacle. Frequently I would see one of them take alarm at a passing flock of starlings and blast off toward the house, then slow abruptly to wend through a narrow corner of the eaves and into an open trapdoor, finally lighting gently on a roost in the cage.

They were skillful, too, I noted, at dropping down off the patio roof. Here they liked to leap out into space, falling free for a moment with wings partially folded, then extending them full out just as they neared the ground, to make a well-timed, braking flutter. It was rather like carrier-based jets using their landing chutes.

As for the windowpanes, the birds had modified their behavior since their accidents. They might still head toward one at full steam, but then, suspecting danger, at the last minute they would veer up or away at right angles (as I winced!) or even pause like a helicopter. Sometimes they would bump the window gently, as though deliberately taking a moderate blow to test the apparent opening without the risk of full collision.

The quail appeared to take great satisfaction in exercising their aeronautical skills, but they were not limited to hedge-hopping or whirly-birding. While they were not speedsters, they could cover short distances rapidly when pressed, particularly with a quick burst from an elevated start. Often they would fly at full speed directly toward some obstacle (such as my head), only to swerve away at the last possible instant. They appeared to know what they were doing and to revel in it. Another amazing technique mastered by both Carrie and Rose involved launching off the ground in a straight burst of powered flight up toward a roof or wall, then folding their wings to coast on up and over in a graceful ballistic trajectory. Like the well-lobbed return of a tennis ball skimming the net, this "catapulted" effect was beautiful to watch, especially going away.

On the other hand, the head-on view of an incoming bird against the clear, blue sky was an aesthetic delight, too. When one of them came sailing silhouetted in on a long, gently curving glide, we were fascinated to see the subtle wing movements and shifts in posture by which they exercised fine control.

Finally, as I became increasingly aware of the pleasure the quail took in flying, I discovered an especially adroit and remarkable performance. Sometimes one of them, apparently for the sheer joy of it, would suddenly drop off a side wall and glide, just off the ground, across the entire length of the yard, slaloming between rocks, shrubs and patio furniture. As she

Carrie can survey the yard from the birdbath or scan the entire neighborhood from a corner of the roof.

skimmed along, she might just brush an occasional wing tip, perhaps deliberately, then finally zoom straight up at the opposite wall to light gracefully on top. It was a striking, artful caper, and we almost felt constrained to applaud when we were treated to it.

Obviously, I was an enthusiastic convert: I had completely revised my view of the quail as ground-bound birds. I was persuaded in fact, that a thorough analysis would show them to be among the best at maneuverability in flight.

Of course, by now I was an unabashed fan of the Gambel's quail in all respects. My appreciation of the breed continued to grow, both for its singular adaptability and for its many other fine qualities. I knew of no species more deserving of our admiration and friendship. And yet, I wondered ironically, could there be any other that had so many enemies?

13

Friends and Enemies

Sometimes it must seem to the Gambel's quail that much of the world is arrayed against them; their natural enemies are remarkably numerous.

To begin with, eggs in the nest are subject to discovery and consequent consumption by a variety of snakes, rodents, large lizards, and foraging skunks. Even ants will occasionally attack the nests, which are particularly vulnerable during hatchout (a chick mustn't take too long in breaking free of his shell). Then come the ravens and the roadrunners; both fancy the taste of the tender young chicks, and either is capable of dispatching an entire brood single-handedly. Finally, there is the constant interest of the coyotes, bobcats, foxes, and especially the "domestic" cats, all of whom maintain a year-round open season on desert quail.

And yet, if the species could name its most formidable enemy, no doubt it would be none of these. The quails' instinctive patterns of protective behavior, and especially their intense natural reaction to danger from the air, all point to yet another skillful predator: their archenemy, the hawk. Indeed, what data we have confirm that the raptors, especially the sharp-shinned and Cooper ("chicken") hawks, are by far the most effective of all in preying upon the Gambel's quail. Appropriately, then, they are also the most feared.

We remembered that Peep-Sight had always been preoccupied with this danger from the sky; it had been evident whenever he was outdoors. It had amused us a little; we could never really take it seriously. Of course, we recognized that such alertness is critical to the quail's survival in the real desert, but the suggestion that a hawk or falcon might come swooping down into our suburban backyard seemed slightly ludicrous.

Our view had carried over to the present brood. As they grew , we watched them refine their initial instinctive caution of all things airborne. First they learned to ignore the butterflies, then later the sparrows (eliminating both as "non-hawks"). We noted, however, their continued apprehension of the larger, long-tailed mockingbird, whose shape is vaguely hawklike. Even after they were grown and bold enough to approach him collectively, the girls remained wary, warning each other whenever he appeared.

Of course, he was no help in making the distinction—he appeared to enjoy the misidentification. I think he came by occasionally just to tease. Finding the quail outside, he was especially pleased if he could spook them into scattering; then he would attempt to mimic their alarm. Soon he was coming by just to demonstrate his skill at it. The quail were not deceived, but I frequently was—upon hearing his mimickry, I would quickly turn and take muster to see who had flown off (no one had).

One day I turned the tables. Spotting him first, I did my imitation of the quails' warning sound, "Kip-kip-kip. . . !" and succeeded in calling their attention to his presence before he had got set to do his routine. He was caught completely by surprise. The girls were gleeful at his discomfiture, and scolded him vociferously as he withdrew in confusion.

While remaining suspicious of the mockingbird, we liked to view the smaller birds as our friends. The truth was that they were little more than free-loaders and hangers-on. During the winter months, we placed seedcakes on the back wall for them. But, never satisfied with these, they came up to the patio, where they could get at the edible litter under and around the girls' cage. They found it more attractive than the seedcakes.

These small birds were sometimes annoying but undiscourageable, and they became tame and numerous. The dowdy English sparrows had little appeal, but the quails' namesakes, the Gambel's sparrows, were neat and perky. They were also especially bold and could hardly wait until I got the girls out each morning so that they could enter the cage and pilfer at will.

The brown field mice lost their caution, too, and many mornings we could look out to see several of them scurrying about beneath the cage in broad daylight, scavenging a breakfast of the millet and canary seed that had fallen through the mesh. Noting our interest, they would zip off across the patio and disappear into the yucca patch.

For the most part, we enjoyed having these little animals around—there was plenty of food for all—and we had only moderate concern that they might infect the quail with something. We felt more apprehensive, however, about the larger visitors that the girls attracted. Occasionally a small dog would crawl under the gate and come around back to investigate. The birds would set up enough racket then to make him nervous or to bring one of us to the rescue. But the dogs never became a serious threat, either.

The occasional cat in the nighttime was another matter. About once a week I could count upon being awakened in the wee hours by a clamor on the patio. I'd hurry out with my flashlight and an ancient air gun, lobbing off an ineffectual B-B at some blur of fur scrambling over the back wall. Then I'd check back to find the birds all in disarray, strewn in extreme positions about the cage where they had lodged as they attempted to scatter. A few reassuring words usually restored order, but now there were feathers everywhere, and I'd suppose that Blacky had made another move.

The feather loss was an interesting phenomenon, perhaps well known to ornithologists but new to us. Apparently a bird, or a Gambel's quail at any rate, will react to a situation in extremis by loosening and losing great numbers of feathers. Presumably this serves to distract his pursuer, after the fashion of a lizard losing its tail. It certainly distracted us—after a series of cat-encounters, some of our birds showed patches of nearly bare skin!

The first time we noticed this effect was on that infamous evening when the adolescent chicks had flown directly from their cage to the corner flower bed, where Blacky the cat had waited to surprise them. Since then, consistently enough, it was often our neighbor Blacky who was responsible again for their feather sheddings. Indeed, for the species as a whole the ultimate enemy may well be the chicken hawk, but for us, the most persistent harassment came from Blacky.

We recognized Blacky early as an adversary to be feared and respected. We frequently saw him in action with the sparrows and lizards; he was shrewd and ruthless, a study in patience and cunning. Well-fed at home, he seldom ate his victims; I suppose he only practiced his ancient art in response to instinctive urgings. Whatever his motivation, he was highly successful.

With the quail, Blacky at first employed the direct approach, assaulting the cage frontally. Failing to break in, he would attempt to capture one of the birds as she sought to force her way out. Soon he concluded that the best time to make this move was in the early morning hours, since it took considerably more ruckus then to rouse us to the defense.

Awakened one morning at 4:00 A.M., I hurried out dazedly to the rescue only to discover that Red-Leg was missing. With our trusty flashlights, Wanda and I made a quick search of roof and ground (predictably unfruitful) and then returned reluctantly to bed. At sunup we began looking again. Soon Wanda had spotted the missing Red-Leg out front, poised on the opposite neighbor's wall. I ambled over to the bird and coaxed her down; then we walked back home together, across the front yards, through the side gate and back around to the patio. Our leader seemed pleased to be home for her breakfast, and our predatory neighbor remained frustrated for the moment.

Although Blacky was identified as our nemesis, I suppose every night-prowling tom in the neighborhood came by now and again to investigate the cage and frighten the girls. No doubt it was great sport. Interestingly, the birds wouldn't call out in alarm when this happened; they simply flew noisily about the cage. I slept lightly, but to be sure I'd hear the girls if they became restless I installed a baby-sitter type intercom from inside the aviary to our bedside. Usually this would rouse me promptly to drive off any reconnoitering night-caller before he actually made his move.

For another preventive measure, I mounted a small floodlight at the front of the cage, with a timer to turn it on each evening. Later I used a photosensitive relay, automatically activating the floodlight as darkness fell and extinguishing it when the sun came up. The birds were very adaptable; they soon became accustomed to the artificial light and slept as soundly as ever. Apparently the illumination did discourage the cats on their early-morning rounds, for the number of predawn awakenings diminished appreciably.

Red-Leg finds her way home at dawn, after fleeing from the cage (to escape Blacky) during the night.

The exception, of course, was Blacky; he was not so easily put off. I'd see him watching us from the wall by day, weighing the whole situation. At night he used the artificial light to his own advantage, lurking in the concealment of the shadows as he contemplated the fully illuminated cage. I could tell he was pondering the quails' behavior—he was especially watchful when they attempted to scatter, as though studying where they went. Eventually, I feared, Blacky would devise some clever way to anticipate them.

I was right. He had slyly noted that in a nocturnal crisis the birds, especially Red-Leg, might force their way out through the trapdoors. Now, unknown to us, he had begun lying in ambush on the patio roof, ready to pounce the moment one came through. We had to admire his cunning and his characteristically masterful execution. He had managed to steal silently across our entire squeaky roof (he had to climb up at the opposite corner), then succeeded in stepping out onto the noisy sheet aluminum over the patio without making a sound. Finally he somehow eased in covertly next to a key niche, only inches away from the roosting Red-Leg. Here he lay patiently waiting for some passing prowler to spook her through and into his grasp.

Fortunately for us Blacky finally tired of waiting, and early one morning he decided to take the initiative, thereby tipping his hand. Aroused through the intercom by the sound of a nervous fluttering, I walked quietly out to the patio door to investigate. Looking up I found myself face to face with Blacky—he was reaching through the niche like a monkey, attempting to open the trapdoor with his paw! The cat and I stared at each other for a moment, eye-to-eye and inches apart; then, with a tremendous tromping and scrambling, he was gone.

Concerned before, I was seriously worried now. Next day I attempted to "cat-proof" the roof with barricades, and in desperation I even electrified the cage. It was all I could think of, but I was still not reassured. Blacky's craftiness and persistence were impressive—perhaps he was just too clever for us. Our counter-measures were a game to him, and eventually he was likely to win. After all, he had little else to occupy his time.

For a while, despite my apprehensions, things remained quiet with no further disturbances from our neighborhood nemesis. Then one Saturday afternoon we were all relaxing in the backyard, with little thought of Blacky, when suddenly one of the birds sounded the hawk warning ("Gerock!?"). All five froze instantly, as required. Knowing that they had learned to ignore the frequent blackbirds, robins, and airplanes, I looked up expecting to see something special. I was not disappointed. Here, incredibly, was a genuine real-live sharp-shinned "chicken" hawk, skimming directly over us at roof-top level! I was amazed at his closeness and chilled at his intense, piercing eyes.

When the birds had relaxed I took them in, but I was grumbling to myself. As if Blacky weren't enough, I thought, now there was this new threat to be guarded against, and apparently it was an important one. Here was a predator swift and bold, and he had clearly noted our location—I felt sure he would be back. For the first time, I began taking the hawk hazard seriously.

Indeed, we saw the hawk frequently thereafter—sometimes perched on the neighbor's roof, watching and waiting; sometimes he actually landed on ours. One day he alighted on our back wall! I was convinced. I could only hope that our training had been effective: if he made a pass at the birds, maybe they would not panic into flying up but would head instead for the cage or the yucca patch. Even so, I feared he would surely capture one of them. The thought sobered me, and when I spoke now about "keeping a sharp eye out for hawks" it was no longer a whimsical remark. From then on, before we took the birds out we made a special point of scrutinizing the neighborhood, checking the walls and roofs, and even scanning the sky for suspicious specks.

It made me wish I had a better way of communicating with the birds; I'd like to be more specific about my warnings. It was just wishful thinking of course. Oh, I could manage the righteous "Rok-chik, Rok-chik!" all right, and I even had some success with the cautioning "Chip-chip-chip?" But other than that the only sure way I knew to send them scurrying off to cover was with a sharp whistle, and this was most likely to leave them confused (apparently it was the grossest type of alarm).

In admonishing each other, of course, the quail were much more skillful and specific than I, able to transmit considerably more than just a basic warning. Their natural language was in fact rather sophisticated, even when dealing with so simple a subject as Friends and Enemies. Certainly their regular day-to-day communications with each other were quite complex, complementing the social structure that they had evolved for themselves. This latter was another whole fascinating area for study and interpretation, and as the sometimes-scientist, I became quite engrossed in observing it. The time spent at it turned out to be most rewarding.

14

Hierarchy

By the time the quail reached maturity, a family structure had developed within the group. In the absence of parents, the five young females had managed by themselves to fill the essential roles of the covey, even those customarily assumed by males. It was yet another example of their remarkable adaptability. After some initial shifting about, each individual appeared to emphasize or develop those characteristics that were most appropriate to her particular assignment.

We had, of course, seen this process taking place earlier, but we had had no idea then where it was leading. Once they were grown, however, and I had an opportunity to watch and record their behavior as adults, I thought I could make sense of what I saw.

The initial arrangement, which remained relatively stable for a time, seemed straightforward enough. It was reflected by this October entry in my notes:

> Although the girls seldom quarrel or bicker, a pecking order of sorts has now evolved among them. At the top, of course, is Red-Leg, clearly in charge but carrying her mantle of leadership casually and not overly impressed with her own importance. She seldom finds it necessary to address one of the others sharply (almost never with a rap on the head!) but does expect a few of the prerogatives of her rank—she takes first priority on mealworms or other goodies, and the uppermost perch is reserved for her daytime dozing.
>
> At the other end of the order is Brownie. This comes as something of a surprise to me, for she is as large and strong as any member of the clan, yet she has permit-

ted herself to become its "whipping boy." As the ultimate recipient of all frustration (when the girls do get irritable and agitated with each other), Brownie is where the pecking stops; she has nowhere to pass it on (except, perhaps, to the sparrows). Oddly, she appears to accept this role with composure and good grace; her reaction is typically one of unruffled tolerance. Certainly, there is nothing in her demeanor to suggest that her sense of worth or self-esteem are affected—quite the contrary, she appears to understand instinctively the value of her function to the group. It occurs to me that the position is recognized as honorable after all, and that it is Brownie's very strength and size that have qualified her for this important slot; a weaker individual might not hold up under such abrasion. In any event, Brownie appears to thrive on it.

Falling between the extremes are Pearl and Rose, apparently in that order, but with less clear distinction between them. This may explain why the altercations we do have generally originate with these two—their arguments are frequent, brief, and largely unresolved.

The most remarkable of all, however, is Carrie, who seems to be *outside* the pecking order altogether. She is somehow entirely off to the side, aloof from hierarchical considerations. As the chief of safety and security, she is presumably immune: she neither pecks nor gets pecked. It is as though she cannot become involved in such activity, lest it somehow interfere with the performance of her important duties.

I liked to refer to Carrie as "the staff person"—she was not a part of any line authority or order of succession, yet somehow she was right next to the leader, a sort of adjutant.

Carrie chooses a characteristic posture for her "portrait."

For a while Red-Leg's spot as top canary went entirely unchallenged, and there was nothing to indicate who might take over if anything should happen to her (it was not likely to be Carrie). Then, finally, the once "dainty and demure" Pearl began to turn her occasional aggressive outbursts toward a surprised Red-Leg. Sure enough, before long Pearl had presumably emerged as next-in-command, and she began exercising a few prerogatives of her own.

Now, so far as we could see, only Rose was left without clearly defined responsibilities. Of course, in our group this in itself constituted a unique position: If the other four were officers and specialists, she alone comprised "the troops."

This is not to say that Rose was without her individual characteristics. She was always the most interested in entering the house and would probably have spent much of her time there if we had permitted it. In the mornings, as I went in and out for feed and water, she invariably sneaked through the door to the kitchen and then explored the other rooms. Typically she would remain inside until I shooed her back out, preferring this to our walks around the yard.

When Chris came home between semesters, Rose took possession of him. Whenever he joined in our outings, she stayed close to him and drove away any of the others who came too near. Her behavior toward them individually reflected the family hierarchy: a mild, buffering motion toward Red-Leg, a somewhat more aggressive reaction to Pearl, and what amounted to aggravated assault upon the phlegmatic Brownie! (Carrie seldom came close.) When Chris left, Rose transferred her apparent infatuation, but with diminished vigor, to one or the other of his brothers, or sometimes to Wanda.

Rose's actions led me to consider again how strongly the birds were imprinted upon us and how we fit into their world. In reflecting upon it, I became convinced that they had remained pretty much a family of quail, that they were not particularly "humanized." They had surely grown up as orphan birds, for even as juveniles they were on their own most of the time. As they matured they appeared to have distributed the elements of the parental roles among themselves, mostly to Red-Leg and Carrie. I suppose that when I was present I preempted some of these. But, even then, Red-Leg appeared to maintain her position as permanent chief; she merely loaned me some of her authority for the moment. Perhaps the birds viewed me as some sort of part-time patriarch—a grandfather or uncle—who came by frequently to guide and guard them as they grew.

It was interesting to note that the formerly independent Red-Leg, once she had reluctantly accepted her role as leader, would now sometimes take clear responsibility for the others. A particular instance was her obvious disapproval whenever we held one of the birds. Occasionally we still had to catch them to renew their markings, and, as we held one, Red-Leg would come up to us and circle about officiously, as though demanding its release. Curiously, if it was Carrie whom we held, Red-Leg pecked at our hands,

Rose at the woodpile.

trying to make us turn her loose; otherwise she was likely to peck at the bird instead! In that case, too, she seemed to chastise the captured bird for submitting; she even followed the freed "delinquent" afterward to make her point with one final peck on the head. But Carrie was a special case and appeared to be inculpable in Red-Leg's eyes.

Oddly, however, while Carrie didn't get scolded by her leader for having been caught, she seemed to take it herself as a personal defeat or humiliation. Sometimes she would mope around afterward as though completely crushed at having permitted it. Her attitude affected me, too, so that I came to dislike especially having to catch and mark her. After one such incident, she acted so dejected that Red-Leg came up repeatedly to console her, walking around and nudging her, apparently encouraging her to resume normal activity. The whole thing depressed me. I resolved then and there to discontinue marking Carrie altogether; I would rely upon other ways to identity this sensitive individual.

Carrie's unique personality and conduct had evolved early and continued to intrigue me. Of all the group, she alone was entirely noncompetitive. On the roosts, she allowed herself to be jostled out of the way without resistance. Her character appeared to involve a certain parental self-denial, an inherent deference to the others; it was as though she must always wait until their needs were met. When I fed the birds mealworms in the cage I tried to see that all got a proper share, but I could seldom get Carrie to take any at all until the others had each had several. When I held one out to her she was slow to accept it, and if another bird approached she would withdraw. After a while, she and I tacitly agreed upon a particular bough as her feeding spot—when she had decided that it was appropriate to partake, she patiently took up her position there and I made a point to respond promptly.

I suppose that Carrie's touching dedication was a necessary adjunct to the effective performance of her group responsibilities. Her role as sentry and watchdog required her to be sober and intent twenty-four hours a day. From the very beginning Carrie had taken her self-appointed job seriously, leaving no time for play or rivalry.

Aside from the peculiarities of Carrie, I became quite engrossed in watching the birds interacting with each other, and I liked to speculate upon its significance. We noticed, for example, that sometimes they seemed to employ standard, stylized behavior patterns. Typically, we characterized these rituals with anthropomorphic designations.

An example was what we called the Curtsey, recalling that classical gesture both in appearance and apparent content. In performing it, the bird faced toward the approaching subject with her legs slightly bent and her wings held out away from her body, quivering rapidly. The message, I think, was one of recognition and deference, and I believe it was supposed to forestall any further approach or assertiveness by the other. The girls often used this on me. We did not believe that it was tied particularly to the mating relationship.

On the other hand, one that we thought could be was the routine we referred to as the Puppy Dog. Here, if one of the birds (or one of us) came suddenly upon another in a particularly vulnerable position, the accosted bird would flatten herself and squeal, rather like a puppy who has had his tail stepped upon. The bird seemed to be pleading not to be hurt, but apparently she did expect to be physically dealt with, for we could readily reach out and pick her up. This, we thought, might be the reaction of a submissive female to a dominant male.

Sometimes a bird wishing to express assertiveness would stretch up tall and beat her wings a few times, accompanying it with a loud "Bleeet!" The gesture seemed to be meant mostly to satisfy her internal needs, for it had little noticeable effect upon others in the vicinity.

One that did, however, was a striking form of dominant-submissive interplay we called Arrest and Custody. This was so extraordinary that if we hadn't observed it carefully on several occasions we should certainly have discounted what we saw as being altogether too improbable. It was most likely to happen when I was returning the birds to their aviary after an outing. Normally Red-Leg waited to be last in, taking a position on the back of an adjacent patio chair, where she could survey the yard and tacitly lend her authority to my ("grandfatherly") efforts at returning the others to the cage. When she saw that I was having too much trouble with one, she might finally hop down and come to my aid, taking the balky bird into the cage herself.

Her technique in this was to stalk purposefully over to the recalcitrant, walking "tall and fluffed out," and escort her deliberately to the entrance. The other bird seemed to understand at once what was involved and immediately fell in alongside. The picture was remarkably like that of an arresting authority leading a truant back to be "booked"—the errant bird was a little self-conscious and stiff, behaving almost as though handcuffed to the officer! There might be a few words of quiet dialogue along the way; then at the step it was up and in without question. The "arrested" bird was now free (in the cage), and Red-Leg returned to her chairback. I found the procedure both remarkable and utilitarian.

Gaining a degree of insight into the hierarchy, the group structure, and the roles of the individual birds was helpful in guiding their activities. Still, my understanding was far from complete. There were times when I got no help at all from Red-Leg, and yet I felt that there was an explanation somewhere close at hand. Rose, for example, behaved well for me—she was always among the first to go in—but with Wanda and the boys she became quite officious and insisted upon staying out to the very last. What was the difference? Many times when the others had all gone in and Red-Leg was about ready to enter, Carrie would come popping back out. Sometimes I lost patience then (frustrated at having come so close to finishing), and resorted to herding or driving them *all* back. I disliked doing this, because it appeared to unsettle the birds—they'd scold and bicker and peck at each other afterward, as though quarreling about whose fault it was that things had gone poorly!

Pearl poses alertly on the back of a patio chair.

After a while I hit upon an idea: Maybe the reason Carrie came back out at this crucial point was to "cover" Red-Leg's entry. When I thought about it, it made sense. As the nominal parent-figure, Red-Leg stood guard while her family returned from the outside world to its home roosts; then Carrie, the professional sentry (and co-parent?), took over so Red-Leg could enter.

It was an interesting theory, and, whether correct or not, recognizing it seemed to help. Now when Carrie came back out, I simply ignored her and waited for Red-Leg to go in. Sure enough, in a moment Carrie would follow along too, and I could close up the cage after all!

My satisfaction with this new insight was short-lived, for the social structure in the covey was still shifting. Now it was Pearl who was in and out, insisting that she be last to enter. I remembered then that Pearl had begun recently to show a special attachment to me. She had made no effort to keep the others away from me, as Rose had done with Chris, but she did stay close at hand whenever we were outside.

It occurred to me that this might explain her unexpected deportment at the cage. Possibly she felt that, by virtue of her attachment, she shared some of my status when I was present. Thus she could be more assertive and entitled to enter last if she chose. (By analogy, this would explain Rose's similar behavior in my absence, when Wanda or the boys were "in charge" of the outings.) The whole thing seemed consistent—status was gained by association with a status figure!

The theory was tantalizing, just begging for further investigation. One could possibly test the concept, I thought, and amplify upon it. Still, I was not comfortable with the prospect. I felt that it would be intruding upon this family of quail unjustifiably—after all, they were not guinea pigs. So I decided to let it pass. It had been enough merely to discover what we knew of the birds' intricate social structure.

And this, we felt, was an impressive system: integrated, comprehensive, adaptive. It appeared to contain a surprising capability for accommodation and self-adjustment. We couldn't help wondering, however, whether it would prove sophisticated enough to withstand the intense internal pressures of an all-female society, once the mating season arrived in full force. Which, of course, it inevitably did.

15

Resolution

Toward the end of February we were all eager for change. We looked hopefully for signs of spring, but winter was reluctant to relinquish its reign. Each morning at our outing the girls clipped off any shoot of daffodil, tulip, or day lily that had managed to push its way up and out of the frosty flower beds. They were ravenous for lettuce and radish tops too, and I knew that they were instinctively seeking the green "winter annuals," rich in vitamin E, that typically emerge in the desert at about this time. These are the natural mechanism that triggers physical changes in the quail, activating their mating behavior.

Eventually it became clear that some such change was taking place anyway, for the birds were becoming quite restless. Now they occasionally paced about in their cage, searching for a way out. It made us uncomfortable to see that they felt restricted, so I took them outside as frequently as I could. Once out, they didn't know what to do. They stayed close to me, as though expecting that I would lead them off at any moment to the common feeding grounds of winter, where they could find the potent little desert annuals (and incidentally, meet new friends).

They readily returned to their cage, but then in a few minutes they would be pacing about again, complaining about their confinement ("Gerock-gerock-gerock") or calling out loudly into the unseen and unhearing world. Their only success in this department was with the chicken hawk, who responded by coming frequently to perch on our rooftop, only a few feet from their cage. We couldn't take them out when he was there, and with their constant calling, he was likely to show up at anytime. In the interests of security, we decided to abandon any thought of leaving the trapdoors open when we were not in attendance, for we were sure that either Blacky or the hawk would take advantage of the situation. Thus, ironically, it was the quails' need for more freedom that finally frustrated our efforts to provide it to them.

We noticed other changes taking place, too. For a few minutes each day Brownie would explore under a particular little blue cypress near the flower beds, making special, soft throaty noises as she poked around. Looking into it, we found a rounded-out, bowl-like spot she may have been considering for a nest. Eventually Pearl, and later Carrie, came to investigate this indenture, making similar comments. Although none of them actually sat in it or spent more than a few minutes there, it appeared to hold a particular interest for all. The girls' increasing restlessness was unmistakable, and we knew that we could not ignore it for long.

One Friday I was driving to work and, as I approached Newton's Corners, I heard a quail call. I pulled over and stopped near a thicket, and in a moment it began again. I recognized the single, mournful call of the male seeking a mate: the one simple, questing "Caa-aw?" repeated every ten or fifteen seconds. Finally, I spotted him silhouetted, solitary and alert, in the leafless upper branches of a mesquite. I knew that the time had come to consider seriously the disposition of the girls. Here, I suspected, was a potentially suitable location.

The Lone Cottonwood, the girls' new home. At right, a calling male at dusk.

That evening we discussed our tentative plan for releasing at least three of our wards, keeping Rose and Pearl, perhaps. We wondered though, whether either group would get along as well as we had thought without the others. Not reaching a conclusion, we agreed to return to the question soon, for the matter had to be resolved shortly.

Next morning while I gave the cage a thorough cleaning, four of the quail went on out through the trapdoors to the roof and then to the yard, as was their custom. Rose stayed behind to kibitz. I climbed inside and overhauled the entire interior—moving the rocks and driftwood around, refilling the seed dispenser, and installing freshly cut boughs. My mind was on our plan, and I failed to notice that this was an especially active Saturday in our area.

Over the back wall there were trucks, trenchers and earth-moving equipment; out front the Power Company was replacing street lights; two doors away our Austrian neighbors were conducting some sort of field trials for Dobermans and Shepherds. The neighborhood virtually thronged with unfamiliar sights and sounds.

Being anxious and jumpy anyway, the quail had soon flown up to the roof tops. Here they could see all the strange activity, and while I continued with my cleaning they called back and forth anxiously and flew to the walls and the neighbors' roofs. I didn't worry about them until I noticed that their clamor had ceased; then the boys came to report that the birds had flown off toward the park. Still not overly concerned, I hosed down the patio and put the aviary in order before going to check on them. Rose (our house quail applicant) had stayed in the cage the whole time, monitoring my efforts and making suggestions as I worked, so now I simply closed her in.

By now it had become a beautiful sunny afternoon, but as I walked toward the park the uncharacteristic noise and traffic was still evident. Three of the missing birds were there, but as I approached they flew to the nearby roof of a vacant house. Here they began calling at length in irregular chorus. Since they were still only a half block or so from home I thought that I might call them back. I returned to climb up on our own roof, where I confidently began, "Chuk-CAW, chuk-CAW, chuk-CAW-caw!" I was encouraged at their enthusiastic replies, recognizing Brownie, Carrie, and Pearl. For a time we stood thus on our respective roofs, calling back and forth, with Rose in the cage below occasionally joining in. The heavy traffic continued, and the dog handlers looked up at me curiously from time to time, but the birds stayed put. Although it seemed to me that we were having a most profound exchange, *they* obviously didn't understand me as saying, "Come on home!"

I gave up, and we all walked back to where the three were perched. It took us several hours to talk them down to the lawn. First we coaxed Pearl close enough to capture, dispatching her immediately (via the boys) back to the cage; then we did the same with Brownie, Wanda carrying her home. Finally I was left with cautious Carrie; of course *she* would never allow herself to be snatched up. With abundant patience, however, and continuing luck, I succeeded in persuading her to walk on home. Down the heavily trafficked street we went, through the now-strange neighborhood, arriving at last at our own front lawn, then around in back and up to the cage.

We had four of the five now, and I suppose we should have been content with that, but we all wished that Red-Leg were here, too—she had been neither seen nor heard since morning. Somehow I was optimistic. I predicted that, if things quieted down, our "leader" would come whirring back before dark.

We didn't have to wait that long. The area was back to normal in another couple of hours, and Rob came to report that our neighbor a few houses away had spotted Red-Leg (he had seen me earlier, walking Carrie home). He was keeping her in view now until I could come to retrieve her.

When I arrived, our considerate friend was talking to the bird in his front yard, keeping her occupied. She casually acknowledged my arrival, and when I invited her to follow me home she came along rapidly. Again, we wended our way across the street and back through the gate to the familiar yard and cage. Here the other quail greeted us effusively, and Red-Leg seemed pleased to be home once more.

One final time we had somehow reassembled this crazy family of five, returning them safe and sound to our backyard. But we concluded then that the time had come to resolve their situation; we couldn't put off their release any longer.

Next morning Wanda and I drove out to Newton's Corners to get the lay of the land. On one quadrant, diagonally opposite Wayne Newton's estate, was a sizeable stretch of empty terrain where I had seen the single calling male. It was a square mile or two of featureless desert—underbrush and thickets—with a few bridle trails. A jeep path led out toward a large patch of especially heavy undergrowth, marked by a single, tall cottonwood. This looked just right to us; if there weren't Gambel's quail in this spot, there certainly should be.

Returning home, we picked up seedcakes, water pans, and a large bag of wild bird seed and loaded them into the car. Finally we were ready; it was time for the final phase of our decision-making. The boys joined in.

We all agreed to the basic idea of setting the covey free at the lone cottonwood; the only question was, who should stay behind? We decided that it should be only one, but who was the best choice? Who was to become our house quail?

We considered each of the girls in turn. Rose, of course, was first to come to mind. Right from the start she had shown a great interest in entering the house, as though she would prefer to live in; no doubt she would adapt well. But Pearl, too, liked the indoors. She had become the stronger personality, and with her recent inclination to identify with me she would surely accommodate readily. Then there was Brownie—although last in the pecking order within the group, she was most interested in people and actually quite outgoing with us. She would be a good choice too. Surprisingly, we found ourselves also thinking quite favorably about Red-Leg, the independent one. We felt that her temperament might actually suit her to the role better than any of the others. Like Peep-Sight, she was quite able to get along on her own, self-sufficient and not missing her "sisters" once they were gone (as in the most recent escapade). Finally, even Carrie was not to be overlooked; she had begun showing some acceptance of people, too, and as guardian of the grounds (again, like Peep-Sight) she might find great fulfillment in the ultimate role as house quail.

We cycled through all the candidates, and after much discussion, we narrowed the choice down to two: Rose and Red-Leg. Which would it be?

Having arrived at this stage, we were able to consider more carefully the various aspects of our selection. We examined them in detail and thereby arrived at a surprising conclusion, as difficult as it was unexpected: There would be no house quail at all. Five had always seemed the right number, we said, and somehow it *still* was—they were a family, and they belonged together. It was a hard decision, but once made, it seemed exactly right. This then, was our resolve: We would set the entire group free, all together, just as they had begun—five of a kind.

After lunch, we collected the birds in the old mouse cage (how they filled it now!) and drove with them out Pecos Road toward Newton's Corners, taking the jeep trail off to the lone cottonwood. Here we set out the bird seed, the water jars, and the seedcakes, and finally we opened the little cage. We watched as the girls stepped out and began eagerly exploring the strange, exciting thicket. They were obviously pleased with it, spreading out in all directions and chattering back and forth, as usual, about their discoveries. This was better than the woodpile! While they were still enthralled, we slipped off quietly toward the car. Rose noticed and began to follow, but we whistled loudly to send her scurrying off into the brush, and before she knew what had happened we had driven away.

It was a quiet house that night and even a little grim the next morning. Stopping by on my way to work (and again in the evening), I was reassured to find that, indeed, a sizeable covey of quail inhabited the exact spot where we had left the girls. Slipping unobtrusively into the mesquite, I could see an apparent leader or sentry, a handsome rooster, who stood up in the branches calling occasionally. There were several others who showed themselves, too, on the ground; I had forgotten how strikingly colorful and proud the males can be. Next day, I saw one of them accompanying a female who certainly could have been Pearl, but I was careful not to intrude.

After a few days of this, Wanda and Mike had to see for themselves. Late on Wednesday afternoon the three of us drove out the jeep trail to the lone cottonwood, hoping to be persuaded once and for all that our girls were "all right."

Arriving at the quiet thicket, we first heard the lone male; soon there were a dozen or so other individuals in the vicinity, making occasional cryptic replies. We listened and watched, and when something started them all calling we were suddenly surrounded by a chorus of "Chuk-CAW-caw's!" Then in the midst of it all, as clear as could be, came the unmistakable "CHUK-CAW-CHIGGA" of Red-Leg! In a moment we heard Pearl, too, and most probably the others as well. We grinned at each other silently. They were there, all right, and already a part of the group.

We stayed a while longer, hoping to catch a glimpse of someone we would recognize, but we could not be certain that we had. Even so, we were encouraged; we felt quite sure that our birds had been assimilated successfully into the wild covey. Somehow, we knew, it had turned out just right. Satisfied, we turned back to the car. Just then we heard a noise in the nearby brush; we paused to see a single female emerging cautiously into view. She studied us carefully, then approached slowly with an occasional inquiring "Chirp?" Soon we could tell it was Rose. She had obviously recognized us, and she came up now and circled around, as though looking for some acknowledgement.

We stood motionless for a moment, but finally we could not contain ourselves, and Wanda said, "Well, Rose, how have you been?" That was all she needed; she began clucking happily about us and followed at our feet when we walked away. As we returned to the car, she stayed close at our heels. It was quite clear—she was not going to be left behind again!

We didn't mind; in spite of everything, this, too, seemed to be just right. Somehow, a difficult decision had been made without us: We were going to have a house quail after all.

Epilogue

From time to time we returned again to the thicket at the lone cottonwood, and we continued to be reassured by what we saw and heard. The quail population there was much larger than we had first thought, and the males, if anything, were in excess. We replenished the girls' "dowry" of bird seed, but it wasn't necessary—the natural food was plentiful.

Later, as I drove to work, I sometimes thought that I saw one of the girls with her mate, alongside the road. And later still, when the broods of chicks began to appear, I couldn't resist speculating on whether any of them were "ours."

Meanwhile Rose settled into the house just as though she had grown up there. We accused her of having "read the book," for she sat on my chair and watched television with us, she took over the top of the highboy, and she even learned to drink Coke from a shot glass. Most remarkable, however, was her persistent effort to fill Peep-Sight's old flower pot with eggs— before giving up, she laid over four dozen!

Rose turned out to be a most remarkable girl, and continued to surprise us with her behavior for some time. But one way or another, I suppose, that is another story.

Addendum

A Note About Orphans and Permits

In Nevada, as in most states, protective legislation provides for strict control of game birds and prohibits their unofficial removal from natural habitats. This rule applies even to cripples, strays, and orphans, requiring that when we come upon these unfortunates, we callously turn our backs upon them. Experience has shown that nature, in the long run, will deal more reasonably with this problem than we do.

Nor is the holder of a Breeder's Permit exempt; he must obtain his stock only from an "approved source," i.e., from another licensed breeder (and not by adopting foundlings, strays, or cripples). On balance, this is a good regulation, preventing numerous abuses.

But are there no exceptions? Must the rule apply even when it is clear that its rigid enforcement will only *assure* deprivation or destruction of the subject, while other alternatives appear to be more humane?

Technically, the answer *has* to be that the law is the law, and there are no exceptions. Furthermore, it is unreasonable to ask a state official to waive the law; he is not empowered to do so (this is reserved to the courts). He is probably as perceptive and compassionate as anyone, but his responsibility is to execute the law, not to grant execeptions to it. The most one can expect from him in such cases is a willingness to look the other way. For our part, we can refrain from inviting his attention unnecessarily.

Finally, with regard to the particular birds in our present story, the reader may be assured that their origin is not likely to be of any official concern today.